THE COMIC ENGLISH GRAMMAR

THE COMIC ENGLISH GRAMMAR

PERCIVAL LEIGH

ISBN: 978-93-5614-124-7

Published: 1840

LECTOR HOUSE LLP
E-MAIL: lectorpublishing@gmail.com

FRONTISPIECE

THE COMIC ENGLISH GRAMMAR;

A NEW AND FACETIOUS INTRODUCTION TO THE ENGLISH TONGUE.

BY

PERCIVAL LEIGH

THE AUTHOR OF THE COMIC LATIN GRAMMAR.

EMBELLISHED
WITH UPWARDS OF FIFTY CHARACTERISTIC
ILLUSTRATIONS BY J. LEECH.

1840.

TO MR. GEORGE ROBINS,

A Writer unrivalled in this or any other Age for

AN ORIGINALITY OF STYLE,

(if the expression may be pardoned) quite unique, and a Dexterity in the Use
of Metaphor unparalleled; whose multifarious and sublime—it would
not be too much to say talented—Compositions would,
it may be fearlessly asserted, afford any

ENTERPRISING PUBLISHER

a not-every-day-to-be-met-with, and not in-a-hurry-to-be-relinquished
opportunity for an

ELIGIBLE INVESTMENT OF CAPITAL,

forming a Property which, under judicious management, would soon become
entitled to the well-merited appellation of a

PRINCELY DOMAIN!

which, without exciting a blush in the mind of veracity, might be said (in a
literary point of view) to be fertilised by a meandering rivulet of Poetry,
comparable for Beauty and Picturesque Effect to

THE SILVERY STREAM OF THE ISIS;

whose richness (equalled only by his fidelity) of description, presenting a
refreshing contrast to the style of his various compeers, precludes the
attempt to perpetrate a panegyric, otherwise than by assuming the
responsibility and risk of applying to him the words of our

IMMORTAL BARD:

"Take him for all in all
We ne'er shall see his like again."

This little Treatise on

COMIC ENGLISH

is, with the most profound Veneration, Admiration, nay, even with
Respect (and the term is used "advisedly") humbly dedicated
by
HIS MOST OBLIGED AND MOST

OBEDIENT SERVANT,
THE AUTHOR.

PREFACE.

It may be considered a strange wish on the part of an Author, to have his preface compared to a donkey's gallop. We are nevertheless desirous that our own should be considered both short and sweet. For our part, indeed, we would have every preface as short as an orator's cough, to which, in purpose, it is so nearly like; but Fashion requires, and like the rest of her sex, requires *because* she requires, that before a writer begins the business of his book, he should give an account to the world of his reasons for producing it; and therefore, to avoid singularity, we shall proceed with the statement of our own, excepting only a few private ones, which are neither here nor there.

To advance the interests of mankind by promoting the cause of Education; to ameliorate the conversation of the masses; to cultivate Taste, and diffuse Refinement; these are the objects which we have in view in submitting a Comic English Grammar to the patronage of a discerning Public. Nor have we been actuated by philanthropic motives alone, but also by a regard to Patriotism, which, as it has been pronounced on high authority to be the last refuge of a scoundrel, must necessarily be the first concern of an aspiring and disinterested mind. We felt ourselves called upon to do as much, at least, for Modern England as we had before done for Ancient Rome; and having been considered by competent judges to have infused a little liveliness into a dead language, we were bold enough to hope that we might extract some amusement from a living one.

Few persons there are, whose ears are so extremely obtuse, as not to be frequently annoyed at the violations of Grammar by which they are so often assailed. It is really painful to be forced, in walking along the streets, to hear such phrases as, "That *'ere* homnibus." "Where've you *bin*." "*Vot's* the *hodds?*" and the like. Very dreadful expressions are also used by draymen and others in addressing their horses. What can possibly induce a human being to say "Gee woot!" "'Mather way!" or "Woa?" not to mention the atrocious "Kim aup!" of the ignorant and degraded costermonger. We once actually heard a fellow threaten to "pitch into" his dog! meaning, we believe, to beat the animal.

It is notorious that the above and greater enormities are perpetrated in spite of the number of Grammars already before the world. This fact sufficiently excuses the present addition to the stock; and as serious English Grammars have hitherto failed to effect the desired reformation, we are induced to attempt it by means of a Comic one.

With regard to the moral tendency of our labours, we may here be permitted to remark, that they will tend, if successful, to the suppression of *evil speaking*.

We shall only add, that as the Spartans used to exhibit a tipsy slave to their children with a view to disgust them with drunkenness, so we, by giving a few examples here and there, of incorrect phraseology, shall expose, in their naked deformity, the vices of speech to the ingenuous reader.

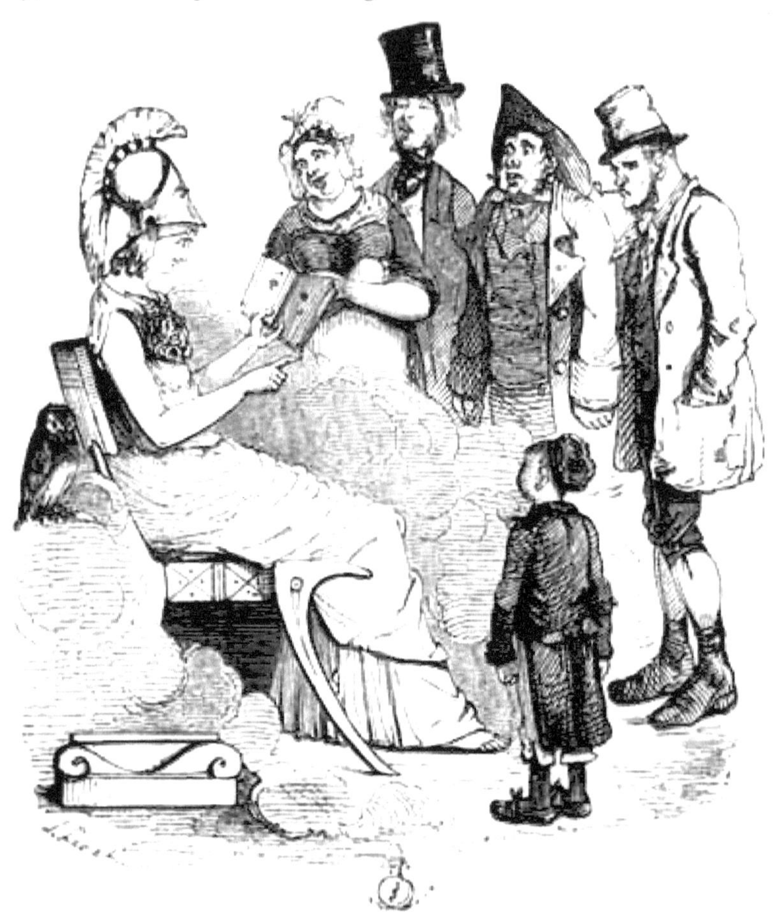

MINERVA TEACHING

CONTENTS

CHAPTER III.

LIST OF ILLUSTRATIONS

PRELIMINARY DISCOURSE.

Our native country having been, from time immemorial, entitled *Merry England*, it is clear that, provided it has been called by a right name, a Comic Grammar will afford the most hopeful means of teaching its inhabitants their language.

That the epithet in question has been correctly applied, it will therefore be our business to show.

If we can only prove that things which foreigners regard in the most serious point of view, and which, perhaps, ought in reality to be so considered, afford the modern Minotaur John Bull, merely matter of amusement, we shall go far towards the establishment of our position. We hope to do this and more also.

Births, marriages, and deaths, especially the latter, must be allowed to be matters of some consequence. Every one knows what jokes are made upon the two first subjects. Those which the remaining one affords, we shall proceed to consider.

Suicide, for instance, is looked upon by Mr. Bull with a very different eye from that with which his neighbours regard it. As to an abortive attempt thereat, it excites in his mind unmitigated ridicule, instead of interest and sympathy. In Paris a foolish fellow, discontented with the world, or, more probably, failing in some attempt to make himself conspicuous, ties a brickbat to his neck, and jumps, at twelve o'clock of the day, into the Seine. He thereby excites great admiration in the minds of the bystanders; but were he to play the same trick on London Bridge, as soon as he had been pulled out of the water he would only be laughed at for his pains.

There was a certain gentleman, an officer in the navy, one Lieutenant Luff; at least we have never heard the fact of his existence disputed; who used to spend all his time in drinking grog; and at last, when he could get no more, thought proper to shoot himself through the chest. In France he would have been buried in Père La Chaise, or some such place, and would have had an ode written to his memory. As his native country, however, was the scene of his exploit, he was interred, for the affair happened some years ago, in a cross-road; and his fate has been made the subject of a comic song.

That our countrymen regard Death as a jest, no one who considers their bravery in war or their appetite in peace, can possibly doubt. And the expressions, "to hop the twig," "to kick the bucket," "to go off the hooks," "to turn up the toes," and so on, vernacularly used as synonymous with "to expire," sufficiently show the jocular light in which the last act of the farce of Life is viewed in Her Majesty's dominions.

An execution is looked upon abroad as a serious affair; but with us it is quite another matter. Capital punishments, whatever they may be to the sufferers, are to the spectators, if we may judge from their behaviour, little else than capital jokes. The terms which, in common discourse, are used by the humble classes to denote the pensile state, namely, "dancing on nothing," "having a drop too much," or "being troubled with a line," are quite playful, and the "Last Dying Speech" of the criminal is usually a species of composition which might well be called "An Entertaining Narrative illustrated with Humourous Designs."

The play of George Barnwell, in which a deluded linendraper's apprentice commits a horrid murder on the body of a pious uncle, excites, whenever it is represented, as much amusement as if it were a comedy; and there is also a ballad detailing the same circumstances, which, when sung at convivial meetings, is productive of much merriment. Billy Taylor, too, another ballad of the same sort, celebrates, in jocund strains, an act of unjustifiable homicide.

Even the terrors of the other world are converted, in Great Britain, into the drolleries of this. The awful apparitions of the unfortunate Miss Bailey, and the equally unfortunate Mr. Giles Scroggins, have each of them furnished the materials of a comical ditty; and the terrific appearance of the Ghost of a Sheep's Head to one William White, — a prodigy which would be considered in Germany as fearful in the extreme, has been applied, by some popular but anonymous writer, to the same purpose. The bodily ablation of an unprincipled exciseman by the Prince of Darkness, a circumstance in itself certainly of a serious nature, has been recorded by one of our greatest poets in strains by no means remarkable for gravity. The appellation, "Old Nick," applied by the vulgar to the Prince in question, is, in every sense of the words, a nickname; and the aliases by which, like many of his subjects, he is also called and known, such as "Old Scratch," "Old Harry," or "The Old Gentleman," are, to say the very least of them, terms that border on the familiar.

In the popular drama of Punch,[1] we observe a perfect climax of atrocities and horrors. Victim after victim falls prostrate beneath the cudgel of the deformed and

[1] It may be said that Punch is a foreign importation. True; and the same assertion may be made respecting the drink of that name, the ingredients of which are all exotic, except the water: nevertheless the peculiar fondness of our countrymen for it will hardly on that account be questioned. But the real fact is, that there is nothing outlandish about Punch except the name, and even that has been Anglicised. We are proverbial for improving on the inventions of other nations, but we have done more than improve upon Punch; we have entirely remodelled his character; and he is now no more an Italian than the descendant of one who came in with the Conqueror is a Norman. The correctness of this position will be found to be singularly borne out on a perusal of that celebrated work, "Punch and Judy;" in which (no doubt from unavoidable circumstances) the dialogues were actually taken down from the mouth of an Italian, one Piccini, an itinerant exhibitor of the drama. The book is, or ought to be, in everybody's hands. Still, let any one refer to that particular part of it, and, provided that his taste is a correct one, he will not fail to be struck with the deteriorating effect which Signor Piccini's broken English and Italian loquacity have produced on the spirit of the original. Nothing is more characteristic of the real Mr. Punch than the laconic manner in which he expresses himself, and nothing at the same time is more English. As to the embellishments of his discourse, introduced by Piccini, they are about as appropriate and admirable as Colley Cibber's improvements on Richard the Third.

barbarous monster; the very first who feels his tyranny being the wife of his bosom. He, meanwhile, behaves in the most heartless manner, actually singing and capering among the mangled carcases. Benevolence is shocked, Justice is derided, Law is set at nought, and Constables are slain. The fate to which he had been consigned by a Jury of his Country is eluded; and the Avenger of Crime is circumvented by the wily assassin. Lastly, to crown the whole, Retribution herself is mocked; and the very Arch Fiend is dismissed to his own dominions with a fractured skull. And at every stage of these frightful proceedings shouts of uproarious laughter attest the delight of the beholders, increasing in violence with every additional terror, and swelling at the concluding one to an almost inextinguishable peal.

Indeed there is scarcely any shocking thing out of which we can extract no amusement, except the loss of money, wherein, at least when it is our own, we cannot see anything to laugh at.

Some will say that we make it a principle to convert whatever frightens other people into a jest, in order that we may imbibe a contempt for danger; and that our superiority (universally admitted) over all nations in courage and prowess, is, in fact, owing to the way which we have acquired of laughing all terrors, natural and supernatural, utterly to scorn. With these, however, we do not agree. Our national laughter is, in our opinion, as little based on principle as our national actions have of late years been. We laugh from impulse, or, as we do everything else, because we choose. And we shall find, on examination, that we have contrived, amongst us, to render a great many things exceedingly droll and absurd, without having the slightest reason to assign for so doing.

For example, there is nothing in the office of a Parish Clerk that makes it desirable that he should be a ludicrous person. There is no reason why he should have a cracked voice; an inability to use, or a tendency to omit, the aspirate; a stupid countenance; or a pompous manner. Nor do we clearly see why he should be unable to pronounce proper names; should say Snatchacrab for Sennacherib, or Leftenant for Leviathan. Such, nevertheless, are the peculiarities by which he is commonly distinguished.

We are likewise at a loss to divine why so studiously ridiculous a costume has been made to enhance the natural absurdity of a Beadle; for we can hardly believe that his singular style of dress was really intended to inspire small children with veneration and awe.

It can scarcely be supposed that a Lord Mayor's Show was instituted only to be laughed at; yet who would contend that it is of any other use? Nor could the office of the Chief Magistrate of a Corporation, nor that of an Alderman, have been created for the amusement of the Public: there is, however, no purpose which both of them so frequently serve.

If the wig and robes of a Judge were meant to excite the respect of the community in general, and the fear of the unconscientious part of it, we cannot but think that the design has been unsuccessful. That the ministers of justice are not, in fact, so reverently held, by any means, as from the nature of their functions they might be expected to be, is certain. A magistrate, to go no further, is universally known, if not designated, by the jocose appellation of "Beak."

Butchers, bakers, cobblers, tinkers, costermongers, and tailors; to say nothing of footmen, waiters, dancing-masters, and barbers have become the subjects of ridicule to an extent not warranted by their avocations, simply considered.

But the comical mind, like the jaundiced eye, views everything through a coloured medium. Such a mind is that of the generality of Britons. We distinguish even the nearest ties of relationship by facetious names. A father is called "Dad," or "The Governor;" an uncle, "Nunkey;" and a wife, "a rib," or more pleasantly still, as in the advertisements, an "encumbrance." Almost every being or thing, indeed, has in English two words to express it, an ordinary and an odd one; and so greatly has the number of expressions of the kind last mentioned increased of late, that, as it appears to us, a new edition of Johnson's Dictionary, enriched with modern additions, is imperatively called for. When we talk of odd words, we have no fear that our meaning will be misunderstood. It is true that there are some few individuals who complain that they do not see any wit in calling a sheep's-head a "jemmy," legs "bandies," or a hand a "mawley;" and it is also true that there was once a mathematician, who, after reading through Milton's Paradise Lost, wanted to know what it all proved?

And now that we are speaking of names, we may mention a few which are certainly of a curious nature, and which no foreigner could possibly have invented; unless, which would be likely enough, he meant to apply them seriously. The names we allude to are names of places—and pretty places they are too; as, "Mount Pleasant," "Paradise Row," "Golden Lane."

Then there are a great many whimsical things that we do:—

When a man cannot pay his debts, and has no prospect of being able to do so except by working, we shut him up in gaol, and humorously describe his condition as that of being in Quod.

We will not allow a man to give an old woman a dose of rhubarb if he have not acquired at least half a dozen sciences; but we permit a quack to sell as much poison as he pleases, with no other diploma than what he gets from the "College of Health."

When a thief pleads "Guilty" to an indictment, he is advised by the Judge to recall his plea; as if a trial were a matter of sport, and the culprit, like a fox, gave no amusement unless regularly run down. This perhaps is the reason why allowing an animal to start some little time before the pursuit is commenced, is called giving him *law*.

When one man runs away with another's wife, and, being on that account challenged to fight a duel, shoots the aggrieved party through the head, the latter is said to receive *satisfaction*.

We never take a glass of wine at dinner without getting somebody else to do the same, as if we wanted encouragement; and then, before we venture to drink, we bow to each other across the table, preserving all the while a most wonderful gravity. This, however, it may be said, is the natural result of endeavouring to keep one another in countenance.

The way in which we imitate foreign manners and customs is very amusing. Savages stick fish-bones through their noses; our fair countrywomen have hoops of metal poked through their ears. The Caribs flatten the forehead; the Chinese compress the foot; and we possess similar contrivances for reducing the figure of a young lady to a resemblance to an hour-glass or a devil-on-two-sticks.

There being no other assignable motive for these and the like proceedings, it is reasonable to suppose that they are adopted, as schoolboys say, "for fun."

We could go on, were it necessary, adducing facts to an almost unlimited extent; but we consider that enough has now been said in proof of the comic character of the national mind. And in conclusion, if any foreign author can be produced, equal in point of wit, humour, and drollery, to Swift, Sterne, or Butler, we hereby engage to eat him; albeit we have no pretensions to the character of a "helluo librorum."

JOHN BULL

THE COMIC ENGLISH GRAMMAR.

"English Grammar," according to Lindley Murray, "is the art of speaking and writing the English language with propriety."

The English language, written and spoken with propriety, is commonly called the King's English.

A monarch, who, three or four generations back, occupied the English throne, is reported to have said, "If beebles will be boets, they must sdarve." This was a rather curious specimen of "King's English." It is, however, a maxim of our law, that "the King can do no wrong." Whatever bad English, therefore, may proceed from the royal mouth, is not "King's English," but "Minister's English," for which they alone are responsible. For illustrations of this kind of "English" we beg to refer the reader to the celebrated English Grammar which was written by the late Mr. Cobbett.

THE "PRODIGY"

He's only a little "prodigy" of mine, Doctor.

King's English (or, perhaps, under existing circumstances we should say, *Queen's* English) is the current coin of conversation, to mutilate which, and unlawfully to *utter* the same, is called *clipping* the King's English; a high crime and misdemeanour.

Clipped English, or bad English, is one variety of Comic English, of which we shall adduce instances hereafter.

Slipslop, or the erroneous substitution of one word for another, as "prodigy" for "protégée," "derangement" for "arrangement," "exasperate" for "aspirate," and the like, is another.

Slang, which consists in cant words and phrases, as "dodge" for "sly trick," "no go" for "failure," and "carney" "to flatter," may be considered a third.

Latinised English, or Fine English, sometimes assumes the character of Comic English, especially when applied to the purposes of common discourse; as "Extinguish the luminary," "Agitate the communicator," "Are your corporeal functions in a condition of salubrity?" "A sable visual orb," "A sanguinary nasal protuberance."

American English is Comic English in a *"pretty particular considerable tarnation"* degree.

Among the various kinds of Comic English it would be *"tout-à-fait"* inexcusable, were we to *"manquer"* to mention one which has, so to speak, quite *"bouleversé'd"* the old-fashioned style of conversation; French-English, that is what *"nous voulons dire." "Avec un poco"* of the *"Italiano,"* this forms what is also called the Mosaic dialect.

English Grammar is divided into four parts—Orthography, Etymology, Syntax, and Prosody; and as these are points that a good grammarian always stands upon, he, particularly when a pedant, and consequently somewhat *flat*, may very properly be compared to a table.

PART I.
ORTHOGRAPHY.

CHAPTER. I.

OF THE NATURE OF THE LETTERS, AND OF A COMIC ALPHABET.

Orthography is like a junior usher, or instructor of youth. It teaches us the nature and powers of letters and the right method of spelling words.

Note.—In a public school, the person corresponding to an usher is called a master. As it is sometimes his duty to flog, we propose that he should henceforth be called the "Usher of the Birch Rod."

Comic Orthography teaches us the oddity and absurdities of *letters*, and the wrong method of spelling words. The following is an example of Comic Orthography:—

islinton foteenth of febuary 1840.

my Deer jemes

wen fust i sawed yu doun the middle and up agin att Vite condick ouse i maid Up my Mind to skure you for my hone for i Felt at once that my appiness was at Steak, and a sensashun in my Bussum I coudent no ways accompt For. And i said to mary at missis Igginses said i theres the Mann for my money o ses Shee i nose a Sweeter Yung Man than that Air Do you sez i Agin then there we Agree To Differ, and we was sittin by the window and we wos wery Neer fallin Out. my deer gemes Sins that Nite i Havent slept a Wink and Wot is moor to the Porpus i Have quit Lost my Happy tight and am gettin wus and wus witch i Think yu ort to pitty Mee. i am Tolled every Day that ime Gettin Thinner and a Jipsy sed that nothin wood Cure me But a Ring.

i wos a Long time makin my Mind Up to right to You for of Coarse i Says jemes will think me too forrad but this bein Leep yere i thout ide Make a Plunge speshialy as her grashius madjesty as Set the Exampel of Popin the queshton, leastways to all Them as dont Want to Bee old Mades all their blessed lives. so my Deer Jemes if yow want a Pardoner for Better or for wus nows Your Time dont think i Behave despicable for tis my Luv for yu as makes Me take this Stepp.

please to Burn this Letter when Red and excuse the scralls and Blotches witch is Caused by my Teers i remain

till deth Yure on Happy
Vallentine
jane you No who.

poscrip

nex Sunday Is my sunday out And i shall be Att the corner of Wite lion Street pentonvil at a quawter pas Sevn.

Wen This U. C.
remember Mee
j. g.

"JANE YOU KNOW WHO"

Now, to proceed with Orthography, we may remark, that

A letter is the least part of a word.

Of a *comic letter* an instance has already been given.

Dr. Johnson's letter to Lord Chesterfield is a capital letter.

The letters of the Alphabet are the representatives of articulate sounds.

The Alphabet is a Republic of Letters.

There are many things in this world erroneously as well as vulgarly compared to "bricks." In the case of the letters of the Alphabet, however, the comparison is just; they constitute the fabric of a language, and grammar is the mortar. The wonder is that there should be so few of them. The English letters are twenty-six in number. There is nothing like beginning at the beginning; and we shall now therefore enumerate them, with the view also of rendering their insertion subsidiary to mythological instruction, in conformity with the plan on which some account of the Heathen Deities and ancient heroes is prefixed or subjoined to a Dictionary. We present the reader with a form of Alphabet composed in humble imitation of that famous one, which, while appreciable by the dullest taste, and level to the meanest capacity, is nevertheless that by which the greatest minds have been agreeably inducted into knowledge.

THE ALPHABET.

A was Apollo, the god of the carol,
B stood for Bacchus, astride on his barrel;
C for good Ceres, the goddess of grist,
D was Diana, that wouldn't be kiss'd;
E was nymph Echo, that pined to a sound,
F was sweet Flora, with buttercups crown'd;
G was Jove's pot-boy, young Ganymede hight,
H was fair Hebe, his barmaid so tight;
I, little Io, turn'd into a cow,
J, jealous Juno, that spiteful old sow;
K was Kitty, more lovely than goddess or muse;
L, Lacooon—I wouldn't have been in *his* shoes!
M was blue-eyed Minerva, with stockings to match,
N was Nestor, with grey beard and silvery thatch;
O was lofty Olympus, King Jupiter's shop,
P, Parnassus, Apollo hung out on its top;
Q stood for Quirites, the Romans, to wit;
R, for rantipole Roscius, that made such a hit;
S, for Sappho, so famous for felo-de-se,
T, for Thales the wise, F.R.S. and M.D.:
U was crafty Ulysses, so artful a dodger,
V was hop-a-kick Vulcan, that limping old codger;
Wenus—Venus I mean—with a W begins,
(*Vell*, if I *ham* a Cockney, *wot* need of your grins?)

X was Xantippe, the scratch-cat and shrew,
Y, I don't know what Y was, whack me if I do!
Z was Zeno the Stoic, Zenobia the clever,
And Zoilus the critic, Victoria for ever!

Letters are divided into Vowels and Consonants.

The vowels are capable of being perfectly uttered by themselves. They are, as it were, independent members of the Alphabet, and like independent members elsewhere form a small minority. The vowels are *a, e, i, o, u,* and sometimes *w* and *y.*

An I. O. U. is a more pleasant thing to have, than it is to give.

A blow in the stomach is very likely to W up.

W is a consonant when it begins a word, as "Wicked Will Wiggins whacked his wife with a whip;" but in every other place it is a vowel, as crawling, drawling, sawney, screwing, Jew. Y follows the same rule.

A consonant is an articulate sound; but, like an old bachelor, if it exist alone it exists to no purpose. It cannot be perfectly uttered without the aid of a vowel; and even then the vowel has the greatest share in the production of the sound. Thus a vowel joined to a consonant becomes, so to speak, a "better half:" or at all events very strongly resembles one.

Consonants are divided into mutes and semi-vowels.

The mutes cannot be sounded *at all* without the aid of a vowel. Like young ladies just "come out," they are silent as long as you let them alone. Some have compared them, on account of their name, to the "Original Good Woman;" but how joining her to anything except to her head again would have cured her of her dumbness, it is not easy to see. *B, p, t, d, k,* and *c* and *g* hard, are the letters called mutes, or, as some have denominated them, *black letters.*

The semi-vowels, which are *f, l, m, n, r, v, s, x, z,* and *c* and *g* soft, have an imperfect sound of themselves. Well! half a loaf is better than no bread.

L, m, n, r, are further distinguished by the name of liquids. Like certain other liquids they are good for mixing, that is to say, they readily unite with other consonants; and flow, as it were, into their sounds.

The specific gravity of liquids can only be rendered amusing by comical *figures.* The gravity, too, of a *solid* is generally the more ludicrous.

A diphthong is the union of two vowels in one sound, as *ea* in heavy, *eu* in Meux, *ou* in stout.

A triphthong is a similar union of three vowels, as *eau* in the word beau; a term applied to dandies, and addressed to geese: probably because they are birds of a feather.

A proper diphthong is that in which the sound is formed by both the vowels: as, *aw* in awkward, *ou* in lout.

MUTES AND LIQUIDS

An improper diphthong is that in which the sound is formed by one of the vowels only, as *ea* in heartless, *oa* in hoax.

According to our notions there are a great many improper diphthongs in common use. By improper diphthongs *we* mean vowels unwarrantably dilated into diphthongs, and diphthongs mispronounced, in defiance of good English, and against our Sovereign Lady the Queen, her crown and dignity.

For instance, the rustics say,—

"Loor! whaut a foine gaal! Moy oy!"

"Whaut a precious soight of crows!"

"As I was a comin' whoam through the corn fiddles (fields) I met Willum Jones."

After this manner cockneys express themselves:—

"I sor (saw) him."

AWKWARD LOUT

"Dror (draw) it out."

"Hold your jor (jaw)."

"I caun't. You shaun't. How's your Maw and Paw? Do you like taut (tart)?"

We have heard young ladies remark,—

"Oh, my! What a naice young man!"

"What a bee—eautiful day!"

"I'm so fond of dayncing!"

Dandies frequently exclaim,—

"I'm postively tiawed (tired)."

"What a sweet tempaw! (temper)."

"How daughty (dirty) the streets au!"

And they also call,—

Literature, "literetchah."

Perfectly, "pawfacly."

Disgusted, "disgasted."

Sky (theatrical dandies do this chiefly) "ske-eye."

Blue, "ble—ew."

We might here insert a few remarks on the nature of the human voice, and of the mechanism by means of which articulation is performed; but besides our dislike to prolixity, we are afraid of getting *down in the mouth*, and thereby going the *wrong way* to please our readers. We may nevertheless venture to invite attention to a few comical peculiarities in connection with articulate sounds.

Ahem! at the commencement of a speech, is a sound agreeably droll.

The vocal comicalities of the infant in arms are exceedingly laughable, but we are unfortunately unable to spell them.

The articulation of the Jew is peculiarly ridiculous. The "peoplesh" are badly spoken of, and not well spoken.

Bawling, croaking, hissing, whistling, and grunting, are elegant vocal accomplishments.

Lisping, as, "thweet, Dthooliur, thawming, kweechau," is by some considered interesting, by others absurd.

Stammering is sometimes productive of amusement.

Humming and hawing are ludicrous embellishments to a discourse. Crowing like a cock, braying like a donkey, *quacking* like a duck, and hooting like an owl, are modes of exerting the voice which are usually regarded as diverting.

But of all the sounds which proceed from the human mouth, by far the funniest are Ha! ha! ha!—Ho! ho! ho! and He! he! he!

HA! HA! HA! HO! HO! HO! HE! HE! HE!

CHAPTER II.
OF SYLLABLES.

Syllable is a nice word, it sounds so much like syllabub!

A syllable, whether it constitute a word or part of a word, is a sound, either simple or compound, produced by one effort of the voice, as, "O!, what, a, lark!—Here, we, are!"

"O!, WHAT, A, LARK!—HERE, WE, ARE!"

Spelling is the art of putting together the letters which compose a syllable, or the syllables which compose a word.

Comic spelling is usually the work of imagination. The chief rule to be observed in this kind of spelling, is, to spell every word as it is pronounced; though the rule is not universally observed by comic spellers. The following example, for the genuineness of which we can vouch, is one so singularly apposite, that although we have already submitted a similar specimen of orthography to the reader, we are irresistibly tempted to make a second experiment on his indulgence. The epistolary curiosity, then, which we shall now proceed to transcribe, was addressed by a patient to his medical adviser.

"Sɪʀ,

"My Granmother wos very much trubeld With the Gout and dide with it my father wos also and dide with it when i was 14 years of age i wos in the habbet of Gettin whet feet Every Night by pumping water out of a Celler Wich Cas me to have the tipes fever wich Cas my Defness when i was 23 of age i fell in the Water betwen the ice and i have Bin in the habbet of Getting wet when traviling i have Bin trubbeld with Gout for seven years

"Your most humbel
"Servent

. . . .

. . . . . .

Cʟᴇᴀʀᴋᴇɴᴡᴇʟʟ"

Chelsea College has been supposed by foreigners to be an institution for the teaching of orthography; probably in consequence of a passage in the well known song in "The Waterman,"

"Never more at Chelsea Ferry,
Shall your Thomas take a *spell*."

Q. Why is a dunce no conjuror?

A. Because he cannot *spell*.

Among the various kinds of spelling may be enumerated spelling for a favour; or giving what is called a broad hint.

Certain rules for the division of words into syllables are laid down in some grammars, and we should be very glad to follow the established usage, but, limited as we are by considerations of comicality and space, we cannot afford to give more than two very general directions. If you do not know how to spell a word, look it out in the dictionary, and if you have no dictionary by you, write the word in such a way, that, while it may be guessed at, it shall not be legible.

CHAPTER III.

OF WORDS IN GENERAL.

There is no one question that we are aware of more puzzling than this, "What is your opinion of *things* in general?" *Words* in general are, fortunately for us, a subject on which the formation of an opinion is somewhat more easy. Words stand for things: they are a sort of counters, checks, bank-notes, and sometimes, indeed, they are *notes* for which people get a great deal of money. Such words, however, are, alas! not English words, or words sterling. Strange! that so much should be given for a mere song. It is quite clear that the givers, whatever may be their pretensions to a refined or literary taste, must be entirely unacquainted with *Wordsworth*.

Fine words are oily enough, and he who uses them is vulgarly said to "cut it fat;" but for all that it is well known that they will not butter parsnips.

Some say that words are but wind: for this reason, when people are having words, it is often said, that "the wind's up."

Different words please different people. Philosophers are fond of hard words; pedants of tough words, long words, and crackjaw words; bullies, of rough words; boasters, of big words; the rising generation, of slang words; fashionable people, of French words; wits, of sharp words and smart words; and ladies, of nice words, sweet words, soft words, and soothing words; and, indeed, of words in general.

Words (when spoken) are articulate sounds used by common consent as signs of our ideas.

A word of one syllable is called a Monosyllable: as, you, are, a, great, oaf.

A word of two syllables is named a Dissyllable; as, cat-gut, mu-sic.

A word of three syllables is termed a Trisyllable; as, Mag-net-ism, Mum-mer-y.

A word of four or more syllables is entitled a Polysyllable; as, in-ter-mi-na-ble, cir-cum-lo-cu-ti-on, ex-as-pe-ra-ted, func-ti-o-na-ry, met-ro-po-li-tan, ro-tun-di-ty.

Words of more syllables than one are sometimes comically contracted into one syllable; as, in s'pose for suppose, b'lieve for believe, and 'scuse for excuse: here, perhaps, 'buss, abbreviated from omnibus, deserves to be mentioned.

In like manner, many long words are elegantly trimmed and shortened; as, or-nary for ordinary, 'strornary for extraordinary, and curosity for curiosity; to which mysterus for mysterious may also be added.

Polysyllables are an essential element in the sublime, both in poetry and in prose; but especially in that species of the sublime which borders very closely on the ridiculous; as,

"Aldiborontiphoscophormio,
Where left'st thou Chrononhotonthologos?"

ALDIBORONTIPHOSCOPHORMIO AND CHRONONHOTONTHOLOGOS

All words are either primitive or derivative. A primitive word is that which cannot be reduced to any simpler word in the language; as, brass, York, knave. A derivative word, under the head of which compound words are also included, is that which may be reduced to another and a more simple word in the English language; as, brazen, Yorkshire, knavery, mud-lark, lighterman.

Broadbrim is a derivative word; but it is one often applied to a very *primitive* kind of person.

PART II.
ETYMOLOGY.

CHAPTER I.

A COMICAL VIEW OF THE PARTS OF SPEECH.

Etymology teaches the varieties, modifications, and derivation of words.

The derivation of words means that which they come from *as words*; for what they come from as *sounds*, is another matter. Some words come from the heart, and then they are pathetic; others from the nose, in which case they are ludicrous. The funniest place, however, from which words can come, is the stomach. By the way, the Lord Mayor would do well to keep a ventriloquist, from whom, at a moment's notice, he might ascertain the voice of the corporation.

Comic Etymology teaches us the varieties, modifications, and derivation, of words invested with a comic character.

Grammatically speaking, we say that there are, in English, as many sorts of words as a cat is said to have lives, nine; namely, the Article, the Substantive or Noun, the Adjective, the Pronoun, the Verb, the Adverb, the Preposition, the Conjunction, and the Interjection.

Comically speaking, there are a great many sorts of words which we have not room enough to particularise individually. We can therefore only afford to classify them. For instance; there are words which are spoken in the *Low Countries*, and are *High Dutch* to persons of quality; as in Billingsgate, Whitechapel, and St. Giles's.

Words in use amongst all those who have to do with horses.

Words that pass between rival cab-men.

Words peculiar to the P. R. where the order of the day is generally a word and a blow.

Words spoken in a state of intoxication.

Words uttered under excitement.

Words of endearment, addressed to children in arms.

Similar words, sometimes called burning, tender, soft, and broken words, addressed to young ladies, and whispered, lisped, sighed, or drawled, according to circumstances.

Words of honour; as, tailors' words and shoemakers' words; which, like the above-mentioned, or lovers' words, are very often broken.

With many other sorts of words, which will be readily suggested by the reader's fancy.

But now let us go on with the parts of speech.

1. An Article is a word prefixed to substantives to point them out, and to show the extent of their meaning; as, *a* dandy, *an* ape, *the* simpleton.

One kind of comic article is otherwise denominated an oddity, or queer article.

Another kind of comic article is often to be met with in Bentley's Miscellany.

2. A Substantive or Noun is the name of anything that exists, or of which we have any notion; as, *tinker, tailor, soldier, sailor, apothecary, ploughboy, thief.*

Now the above definition of a substantive is Lindley Murray's, not ours. We mention this, because we have an objection, though, not, perhaps, a serious one, to urge against it; for, in the first place, we have "no notion" of impudence, and yet impudence is a substantive; and, in the second, we invite attention to the following piece of Logic,

> A substantive is something,
> But nothing is a substantive;
> Therefore, nothing is something.

A substantive may generally be known by its taking an article before it, and by its making sense of itself: as, a *treat*, the *mulligrubs*, an *ache*.

3. An Adjective is a word joined to a substantive to denote its quality; as a *ragged* regiment, an *odd* set.

You may distinguish an adjective by its making sense with the word thing: as, a *poor* thing, a *sweet* thing, a *cool* thing; or with any particular substantive, as a *ticklish* position, an *awkward* mistake, a *strange* step.

4. A Pronoun is a word used in lieu of a noun, in order to avoid tautology: as, "The man wants calves; *he* is a lath; *he* is a walking-stick."

5. A Verb is a word which signifies to be, to do, or to suffer: as, I am; I calculate; I am fixed.

A verb may usually be distinguished by its making sense with a personal pronoun, or with the word *to* before it: as I *yell*, he *grins*, they *caper*; or to *drink*, to *smoke*, to *chew*.

Fashionable accomplishments!

Certain substantives are, with peculiar elegance, and by persons who call themselves *genteel*, converted into verbs: as, "Do you *wine*?" "Will you *malt*?" "Let me persuade you to *cheese*?"

6. An Adverb is a part of speech which, joined to a verb, an adjective, or another adverb, serves to express some quality or circumstance concerning it: as, "She swears *dreadfully*; she is *incorrigibly* lazy; and she is *almost continually* in liquor."

7. An adverb is generally characterised by answering to the question, How? how much? when? or where? as in the verse, "*Merrily* danced the Quaker's wife," the answer to the question, How did she dance? is, merrily.

8. Prepositions serve to connect words together, and to show the relation be-

tween them: as,

"Off *with* his head, so much *for* Buckingham!"

9. A Conjunction is used to connect not only words, but sentences also: as, Smith *and* Jones are happy *because* they are single. A miss is *as* good *as* a mile.

SINGLE BLESSEDNESS

10. An Interjection is a short word denoting passion or emotion: as, "*Oh*, Sophonisba! Sophonisba, *oh!*" Pshaw! Pish! Pooh! Bah! Ah! Au! Eughph! Yah! Hum! Ha! Lauk! La! Lor! Heigho! Well! There! &c.

Among the foregoing interjections there may, perhaps, be some unhonoured by the adoption of genius, and unknown in the domains of literature. For the present notice of them some apology may be required, but little will be given; their insertion may excite astonishment, but their omission would have provoked complaint: though unprovided with a Johnsonian title to a place in the English vocabulary, they have long been recognised by the popular voice; and let it be remembered, that as custom supplies the defects of legislation, so that which is not sanctioned by magisterial authority may nevertheless be justified by vernacular usage.

CHAPTER II.

OF THE ARTICLES.

The Articles in English are two, *a* and *the*; *a* becomes *an* before a vowel, and before an *h* which is not sounded: as, *an* exquisite, *an* hour-glass. But if the *h* be pronounced, the *a* only is used: as, *a* homicide, *a* homœopathist, *a* hum.

This rule is reversed in what is termed the Cockney dialect: as, *a* inspector, *a* officer, *a* object, *a* omnibus, *a* individual, *a* alderman, *a* honour, *an* horse, or rather, a *norse*, *an* hound, *an* hunter, &c.

It is usual in the same dialect, when the article *an* should, in strict propriety, precede a word, to omit the letter *n*, and further, for the sake of euphony and elegance, to place the aspirate *h* before the word; as, a *hegg*, a *haccident*, a *hadverb*, a *hox*. But sometimes, when a word begins with an *h*, and has the article *a* before it, the aspirate is omitted, the letter *a* remaining unchanged: as, a '*ogg*, a '*edge*, a '*emisphere*, a '*ouse*.

The slight liberties which it is the privilege of the people to take with the article and aspirate become always most evident in the expression of excited feeling, when the stress which is laid upon certain words is heightened by the peculiarity of the pronunciation: as, "You *hignorant hupstart!* you *hilliterate* '*og!* '*ow* dare you to *hoffer* such a *hinsult* to my *hunderstanding?* — You are a *hobject* of contempt, you *hare*, and a *hinsolent wagobond!* your mother was nothing but a *happle-woman*, and your father was an '*uckster!*"

Note. — In the above example, the ordinary rules of language relative to the article and aspirate (to say nothing of the maxims of politeness) are completely set at nought; but it must be remembered, that in common discourse the modification of the article, and the omission or use of the aspirate, are determined by the Cockneys according to the ease with which particular words are pronounced; as, "Though *himpudent*, he warn't as *impudent* as Bill wur." Here the word *impudent*, following a vowel-sound, is most easily pronounced as *himpudent*, while the same word, coming after a consonant, even in the same sentence, is uttered with greater facility in the usual way.

A or *an* is called the indefinite article, because it is used, in a vague sense, to point out some one thing belonging to a certain kind, but in other respects indeterminate; as,

"*A* horse, *a* horse, my kingdom for *a* horse!"

So say grammarians. Eating-house keepers tell a different story. A cheese, in common discourse, means an object of a certain shape, size, weight, and so on, entire and perfect; so that to call half a cheese a cheese, would constitute a flaw in an indictment against a thief who had stolen one. But a waiter will term a fraction, or a modicum of cheese, *a* cheese; a plate-full of pudding, *a* pudding; and *a* stick of celery, a celery, or rather, a *salary*. Nay, he will even apply the article *a* to a word which does not stand for an individual object at all; as *a* bread, *a* butter, *a* bacon. Here we are reminded of the famous exclamation of one of these gentry: — "Master! master! there's two teas and a brandy-and-water just hopped over the palings!"

The is termed the definite article, inasmuch as it denotes what particular thing or things are meant; as,

> "*The* miller he stole corn,
> *The* weaver he stole yarn,
> And *the* little tailòr he stole broad-cloth
> To keep *the* three rogues warm."

A substantive to which no article is prefixed is taken in a general sense; as, "Apple sauce is proper for goose;" that is, for all geese.

APPLE-SAUCE

A few additional remarks may advantageously be made with respect to the articles. The mere substitution of the definite for the indefinite article is capable of changing entirely the meaning of a sentence. "That is *a* ticket" is the assertion of a certain fact; but "That is *the* ticket!" means something which is quite different.

The article is not prefixed to a proper name; as, Stubbs, Wiggins, Chubb, or Hobson, except for the sake of distinguishing a particular family, or description of persons; as, He is *a* Burke; that is, one of the Burkes, or *a* person resembling Burke. The article is sometimes also prefixed to a proper name, to point out some distinguished individual; as, *The* Burke, or the great politician, or the resurrectionist, Burke.

Who is *the* Smith?

The indefinite article is joined to substantives in the singular number only. We have heard people say, however, "He keeps *a* wine-vaults;" or, to quote more correctly — waltz. The definite article may be joined to plurals also.

The definite article is frequently used with adverbs in the comparative and superlative degree: as, "*The* longer I live, *the* broader I grow;" or, as we have all heard the showman say, "This here, gentlemen and ladies, is the vonderful heagle of the sun; *the* 'otterer it grows, *the* higherer he flies!"

CHAPTER III.

SUBSTANTIVES, GENDER, NUMBER, CASE.

SECTION I.
OF SUBSTANTIVES IN GENERAL.

Substantives are either proper or common.

Proper names, or substantives, are the names belonging to individuals: as William, Birmingham.

These are sometimes converted into nicknames, or *improper* names: as Bill, Brummagem.

Common names, or substantives, denote kinds containing many sorts, or sorts containing many individuals under them: as brute, beast, bumpkin, cherub, infant, goblin, &c.

Proper names, when an article is prefixed to them, are employed as common names: as, "They thought him a perfect *Chesterfield*; he quite astonished the *Browns*."

Common names, on the other hand, are made to denote individuals, by the addition of articles or pronouns: as,

"There was *a* little man, and he had *a* little gun."

"*That* boy will be the death of me!"

Substantives are considered according to gender, number, and case; they are all of the third person when spoken *of*, and of the second when spoken *to*: as,

> Matilda, fairest maid, who art
> In countless bumpers toasted,
> O let thy pity baste the heart
> Thy fatal charms have roasted!

SECTION II.
OF GENDER.

The distinction between nouns with regard to sex is called Gender. There are three genders; the Masculine, the Feminine, and the Neuter.

The masculine gender belongs to animals of the male kind: as, a fop, a jackass, a boar, a poet, a lion.

The feminine gender is peculiar to animals of the female kind: as, a poetess, a lioness, a goose.

MATILDA

The neuter gender is that of objects which are neither males nor females: as, a toast, a tankard, a pot, a pipe, a pudding, a pie, a sausage, a roll, a muffin, a crumpet, a puff, a cheesecake, a bun, an apricot, an orange, a lollipop, a cream, an ice, a jelly, &c. &c. &c.

We might go on to enumerate an infinity of objects of the neuter gender, of all sorts and kinds; but in the selection of the foregoing examples we have been guided by two considerations:—

1. The desire of exciting agreeable emotions in the mind of the reader.

2. The wish to illustrate the following proposition, "That almost everything nice is also neuter."

Except, however, a nice young lady, a nice duck, and one or two other nice things, which we do not at present remember.

Some neuter substantives are by a figure of speech converted into the masculine or feminine gender: thus we say of the sun, that when *he* shines upon a Socialist, he shines upon a thief; and of the moon, that she affects the minds of lovers.

A SOCIALIST

There are certain nouns with which notions of strength, vigour, and the like qualities, are more particularly connected; and these are the neuter substantives which are figuratively rendered masculine. On the other hand, beauty, amiability, and so forth, are held to invest words with a feminine character. Thus the sun is said to be masculine, and the moon feminine. But for our own part, and our view is confirmed by the discoveries of astronomy, we believe that the sun is called masculine from his supporting and sustaining the moon, and finding her the wherewithal to shine away as she does of a night, when all quiet people are in bed; and from his being obliged to keep such a family of stars besides. The moon, we think, is accounted feminine, because she is thus maintained and kept up in her splendour, like a fine lady, by her husband the sun. Furthermore, the moon is continually changing; on which account alone she might be referred to the feminine gender. The earth is feminine, tricked out, as she is, with gems and flowers. Cities and towns are likewise feminine, because there are as many windings, turnings, and little odd corners in them as there are in the female mind. A ship is feminine, inasmuch as she is blown about by every wind. Virtue is feminine by courtesy. Fortune and *mis*fortune, like mother and daughter, are both feminine. The Church is feminine, because she is married to the state; or married to the state because she is feminine—we do not know which. Time is masculine, because he is so trifled with by the ladies.

"SHAN'T I SHINE TO-NIGHT, DEAR?"

The English language distinguishes the sex in three manners; namely,

1. By different words; as,

MALE.	FEMALE.
Bachelor	Maid.
Boar	Sow.
Boy	Girl.
Bull	Cow.

Brother	Sister.
Buck	Doe.
Bullock	Heifer.
Hart	Roe.
Cock	Hen.
Dog	Bitch.
Drake	Duck.
Wizard	Witch.
Earl	Countess.
Father	Mother.
Friar	Nun.

And several other

> Words we don't mention,
> (Pray pardon the crime,)
> Worth your attention,
> But wanting in rhyme.

2. By a difference of termination; as,

MALE.	FEMALE.
Poet	Poetess.
Lion	Lioness, &c.

3. By a noun, pronoun, or adjective being prefixed to the substantive; as,

MALE.	FEMALE.
A cock-lobster	A hen-lobster.
A jack-ass	A jenny-ass (vernacular).
A man-servant, or flunkey.	A maid-servant, or Abigail.
A he-bear (like King Harry).	A she-bear (like Queen Bess).
A male flirt (a rare animal).	A female flirt (a common animal).

We have heard it said, that every Jack has his Jill. That may be; but it is by no means true that every cock has his hen; for there is a

> Cock-swain, but no Hen-swain.
> Cock-eye, but no Hen-eye.
> Cock-ade, but no Hen-ade.
> Cock-atrice, but no Hen-atrice.
> Cock-horse, but no Hen-horse.
> Cock-ney, but no Hen-ney.

Then we have a weather-cock, but no weather-hen; a turn-cock, but no turn-hen; and many a jolly cock, but not one jolly hen; unless we except some of those by whom their mates are pecked.

Some words; as, parent, child, cousin, friend, neighbour, servant, and several others, are either male or female, according to circumstances. The word blue (used as a substantive) is one of this class.

It is a great pity that our language is so poor in the terminations that denote gender. Were we to say of a woman, that she is a rogue, a knave, a scamp, or a vagabond, we feel that we should use, not only strong but improper expressions. Yet we have no corresponding terms to apply, in case of necessity, to the female. Why is this? Doubtless because we never want them. For the same reason, our forefathers transmitted to us the words, philosopher, astronomer, philologer, and so forth, without any feminine equivalent. Alas! for the wisdom of our ancestors! They never calculated on the March of Intellect.

We understand that it is in contemplation to coin a new word, *memberess*; it being confidently expected that by the time the new Houses of Parliament are finished, the progress of civilisation will have furnished us with female representatives.

In that case the House will be an assembly of *Speakers*.

But if all the old women are to be turned out of St. Stephen's, and their places to be filled with young ones, the nation will hardly be a loser by the change.

SECTION III.
OF NUMBER.

Number is the consideration of an object as one or more; as, one *poet*, two, three, four, five *poets*; and so on, ad infinitum.

Other countries may reckon up as many poets as they please; England has *one more*.

The singular number expresses one object only; as, a towel, a viper.

The plural signifies more objects than one; as, towels, vipers.

Some nouns are used only in the singular number; dirt, pitch, tallow, grease, filth, butter, asparagus, &c.; others only in the plural; as, galligaskins, breeches, &c.

Some words are the same in both numbers; as, sheep, swine, and some others.

> "A doctor, both to sheep and swine,"
> Said Mrs. Glass, "I am;
> For legs of mutton I can *dress,*
> And shine in *curing* ham."

The plural number of nouns is usually formed by adding s to the singular; as, dove, doves, love, loves, &c.

> Julia, *dove* returns to *dove,*
> Quid pro quo, and *love* for *love*;

Happy in our mutual *loves*,
Let us live like turtle *doves*!

JULIA

When, however, the substantive singular ends in x, ch *soft*, sh, ss, or s, we add es in the plural.

But remember, though box
In the plural makes boxes,
That the plural of ox
Should be *oxen*, not *oxes*.

A few *Singular Plurals*, or Plurals popularly varied, are as follow:—

SINGULAR.	PLURAL.
Beast	Beastes, beastices.
Crust	Crustes.
Gust	Gustes.

Ghost	Ghostes.
Host	Hostes.
Joist	Joistes.
Mist	Mistes.
Nest	Nestes.
Post, &c.	Postes, postices, &c.

Note. — The singular is often used, by a kind of licence conceded to persons of refinement, for the plural; as, "May I trouble you for *a bean*?" "Will you assist Miss Spriggins to *a pea*?" So also people say, "A few *green*." "Two or three *radish*," &c.

SECTION IV.
OF CASE.

There is nearly as much difference between Latin and English substantives, with respect to the number of cases pertaining to each, as there is between a quack-doctor and a physician; for while in Latin substantives have six cases, in English they have but three. But the analogy should not be strained too far; for the fools in the world (who furnish the quack with his cases) more than double the number of the wise.

A VERY BAD CASE

The cases of substantives are these: the Nominative, the Possessive or Genitive, and the Objective or Accusative.

The Nominative Case merely expresses the name of a thing, or the subject of the verb: as, "The doctors differ;" — "The patient dies!"

Possession, which is nine points of the law, is what is signified by the Possessive Case. This case is distinguished by an apostrophe, with the letter s subjoined to it: as, "My soul's idol!" — "A pudding's end."

But when the plural ends in *s*, the apostrophe only is retained, and the other *s* is omitted: as, "The Ministers' Step;" — "The Rogues' March;" — "Crocodiles' tears;" — "Butchers' mourning."

When the singular terminates in *ss*, the letter *s* is sometimes, in like manner, dispensed with: as, "For goodness' sake!" — "For righteousness' sake!" Nevertheless, we have no objection to "Guinness's" Stout.

The Objective Case follows a verb active, and expresses the object of an action, or of a relation: as, "Spring beat Bill;" that is, Bill or "William *Neate*." Hence, perhaps, the American phrase, "I'll lick you *elegant*."

By the by, it seems to us, that when the Americans revolted from the authority of England, they determined also to revolutionise their language.

The Objective Case is also used with a preposition: as, "You are in a mess."

English substantives may be declined in the following manner: —

SINGULAR.

What is the nominative case
Of her who used to wash your face,
Your hair to comb, your boots to lace?
A *mother*!

What the possessive? Whose the slap
That taught you not to spill your pap,
Or to avoid a like mishap?
A *mother's*!

And shall I the objective show?
What do I hear where'er I go?
How is your? — whom they mean I know,
My *mother*!

PLURAL.

Who are the anxious watchers o'er
The slumbers of a little bore,
That screams whene'er it doesn't snore?
Why, *mothers*!

Whose pity wipes its piping eyes,
And stills maturer childhood's cries,
Stopping its mouth with cakes and pies?

Oh! *mothers'*!

And whom, when master, fierce and fell,
Dusts truant varlets' jackets well,
Whom do they, roaring, run and tell?
Their *mothers*!

CHAPTER IV.

OF ADJECTIVES.

SECTION I.
OF THE NATURE OF ADJECTIVES AND THE DEGREES OF COMPARISON.

An English Adjective, whatever may be its gender, number, or case, like a rusty weathercock, never varies. Thus we say, "A certain cabinet; certain rogues."

But as a rusty weathercock may vary in being more or less rusty, so an adjective varies in the degrees of comparison.

The degrees of comparison, like the genders, the Graces, the Fates, the Kings of Cologne, the Weird Sisters, the Jolly Postboys, and many other things, are three; the Positive, the Comparative, and the Superlative.

The Positive state simply expresses the quality of an object; as, fat, ugly, foolish.

The Comparative degree increases or lessens the signification of the positive; as, fatter, uglier, more foolish, less foolish.

The Superlative degree increases or lessens the positive to the highest or lowest degree; as, fattest, ugliest, most foolish, least foolish.

Amongst the ancients, Ulysses was the *fattest*, because nobody could *compass* him.

Aristides the Just was the *ugliest*, because he was so very *plain*.

The most *foolish*, undoubtedly, was Homer; for who was more *natural* than he?

The positive becomes the comparative by the addition of *r* or *er*; and the superlative by the addition of *st* or *est* to the end of it; as, brown, browner, brownest; stout, stouter, stoutest; heavy, heavier, heaviest; wet, wetter, wettest. The adverbs *more* and *most*, prefixed to the adjective, also form the superlative degree; as, heavy, more heavy, most heavy.

Most heavy is the drink of draymen: hence, perhaps, the *weight* of those important personages. More of this, however, in our forthcoming work on Phrenology.

Monosyllables are usually compared by *er* and *est*, and dissyllables by *more* and *most*; except dissyllables ending in *y* or in *le* before a mute, or those which are accented on the last syllable; for these, like monosyllables, easily admit of *er* and *est*. But these terminations are scarcely ever used in comparing words of more than two syllables.

We have some words, which, from custom, are irregular in respect of comparison; as, good, better, best; bad, worse, worst, &c. Much amusement may be derived from the comparisons of adjectives, as made by natural grammarians; a class of beings who generally inhabit the kitchen or stable, but may sometimes be met with in more elevated regions. A few examples will not be out of place. We are not speaking of *servants*, but of degrees of comparison; as,

POSITIVE.	COMPARATIVE.	SUPERLATIVE.
Good	More better, betterer or more betterer.	Most best, bestest.
Tight	More tighter, tighterer or more tighterer.	Most tightest.
Bad	Wuss or wusser.	Wust or wussest.
Handsome	More handsomer like.	Most handsomest.
Extravagant	Extravaganter, more extravaganter.	Extravagantest, most extravagantest.
Stupid	Stupider, more stupider.	Stupidest, most stupidest.
Little	Littler, more littler.	Littlest, most littlest.

With many others.

Here also may be adduced the Yankee's "notion" of comparison; "My uncle's a tarnation rogue; but I'm a tarnation*er*."

SECTION II.
A FEW REMARKS ON THE SUBJECT OF COMPARISON.

Comparisons appear to have been strongly disapproved of by Dr. Johnson. "Sir," said he, "the Whigs make comparisons." It must be confessed that the Doctor's meaning is not quite so evident here as it is in general; but that may be the fault of his biographer. Perhaps some of the Whigs had been making comparisons at his expense, or impertinent comparisons, which his temper, being *positive*, may have tempted them to indulge in. Or they may have been *out* in making their comparisons, which, in that case, must of course have been bad. But a truce to speculations of this kind, on the saying of one, another of whose dogmas was, that "the man who could make a pun would also pick a pocket." We only hope, that such comparisons as we may make, will no more vex his spirit now than they would once have aroused his bile.

Lindley Murray judiciously observes, that "if we consider the subject of comparison attentively, we shall perceive that the degrees of it are infinite in number, or at least indefinite:" and he proceeds to say, "A mountain is larger than a mite; by how many degrees? How much bigger is the earth than a grain of sand? By how many degrees was Socrates wiser than Alcibiades? or by how many is snow whiter than this paper? It is plain," quoth Lindley, "that to these and the like questions no definite answers can be returned."

No; but an impertinent one may. Ask the first charity-boy you meet any one of them, and see if he does not immediately respond, "Ax my eye;" or, "As much again as half."

But when quantity can be exactly measured, the degrees of excess may be exactly ascertained. A foot is just twelve times as long as an inch; a tailor is nine times less than a man.

Moreover, to compensate for the indefiniteness of the degrees of comparison, we use certain adverbs and words of like import, whereby we render our meaning tolerably intelligible; as, "Byron was a *much* greater poet than Muggins." "Honey is *a great deal* sweeter than wax." "Sugar is *considerably* more pleasant than the cane." "Maria says, that Dick the butcher is *by far* the most killing young man she knows."

The words very, exceedingly, and the like, placed before the positive, give it the force of the superlative; and this is called by some the superlative of eminence, as distinguished from the superlative of comparison. Thus, Very Reverend is termed the superlative of eminence, although it is the title of a dean, not of a cardinal; and Most Reverend, the appellation of an Archbishop, is called the superlative of comparison.

A *Bishop*, in our opinion, is *Most Excellent*.

The comparative is sometimes so employed as to express the same pre-eminence or inferiority as the superlative. For instance; the sentence, "Of all the cultivators of science, the botanist is the most crafty," has the same meaning as the following "The botanist is more crafty than any other cultivator of science."

Why? some of our readers will ask—

Because he is acquainted with all sorts of *plants*.

CHAPTER V.
OF PRONOUNS.

Pronouns or proxy-nouns are of three kinds; namely, the Personal, the Relative, and the Adjective Pronouns.

Note.—That when we said, some few pages back, that a pronoun was a word used instead of a noun, we did not mean to call such words as thingumibob, what-siname, what-d'ye-call-it, and the like, pronouns.

And that, although we shall proceed to treat of the pronouns in the English language, we shall have nothing to do, at present, with what some people please to call pronoun-*ciation*.

SECTION I.
OF THE PERSONAL PRONOUNS.

"Mr. Haddams, don't be personal, Sir!"

"I'm not, Sir."

"You har, Sir!"

"What did I say, Sir?—tell me that."

"You reflected on my perfession, Sir; you said, as there was *some* people as always stuck up for the *cloth*; and you insinnivated that certain parties dined off *goose* by means of *cabbaging* from the parish. I ask any gentleman in the westry, if that an't personal?"

"Vell, Sir, vot I says I'll stick to."

"Yes, Sir, like vax, as the saying is."

"Wot d'ye mean by that, Sir?"

"Wot I say, Sir!"

"You're a individual, Sir!"

"You're another, Sir!"

"You're no gentleman, Sir!"

"You're a humbug, Sir!"

"You're a knave, Sir!"

"You're a rogue, Sir!"

A SELECT VESTRY

"You're a wagabond, Sir!"

"You're a willain, Sir!"

"You're a tailor, Sir!"

"You're a cobbler, Sir!" (Order! order! chair! chair! &c.)

The above is what is called personal language. How many different things one word serves to express in English! A pronoun may be as personal as possible, and yet nobody will take offence at it.

There are five Personal Pronouns; namely, I, thou, he, she, it; with their plurals, we, ye or you, they.

Personal Pronouns admit of person, number, gender, and case.

Pronouns have three persons in each number.

In the Singular;

I, is the first person.

Thou, is the second person.

He, she, or it, is the third person.

In the plural;

We, is the first person.

Ye or you, is the second person.

They, is the third person.

This account of persons will be very intelligible when the following Pastoral Fragment is reflected on: —

HE.

I love thee, Susan, on my life:
Thou art the maiden for a wife.
He who lives single is an ass;
She who ne'er weds a luckless lass.
It's tiresome work to live alone;
So come with me, and be my own.

SHE.

We maids are oft by men deceived;
Ye don't deserve to be believed;
You don't—but there's my hand—heigho!
They tell us, women can't say no!

The speaker or speakers are of the first person; those spoken to, of the second; and those spoken of, of the third.

Of the three persons, the first is the most universally admired.

The second is the object of much adulation and flattery, and now and then of a little abuse.

The third person is generally made small account of; and, amongst other grievances, suffers a great deal from being frequently bitten about the back.

The Numbers of pronouns, like those of substantives, are, as we have already seen, two; the singular and the plural.

In addressing yourself to anybody, it is customary to use the second person plural instead of the singular. This practice most probably arose from a notion, that to be thought twice the man that the speaker was, gratified the vanity of the person addressed. Thus, the French put a double Monsieur on the backs of their letters.

Editors say "We," instead of "I," out of modesty.

The Quakers continue to say "thee" and "thou," in the use of which pronouns, as well as in the wearing of broad-brimmed hats and of stand-up collars, they perceive a peculiar sanctity.

Gender has to do only with the third person singular of the pronouns, he, she, it. He is masculine; she is feminine; it is neuter.

Pronouns have the like cases with substantives; the nominative, the possessive, and the objective.

Would that they were the hardest cases to be met with in this country!

The personal pronouns are thus declined:—

CASE.	FIRST PERSON SINGULAR.	FIRST PERSON PLURAL.
Nom.	I	We.
Poss.	Mine	Ours.
Obj.	Me	Us.

Pronouns, you see, are declined without fuss.

CASE.	SECOND PERSON.	SECOND PERSON.
Nom.	Thou	Ye or you.
Poss.	Thine	Yours.
Obj.	Thee	You.

How glad I shall be when my task I've got through!

Now the third person singular, as we before observed, has genders; and we shall therefore decline it in a different way. Variety is charming.

THIRD PERSON SINGULAR.

CASE.	MASC.	FEM.	NEUT.
Nom.	He	She	It.
	Well	done	Kit!
Poss.	His.	Hers	Its.
	Now	Tom's	quits.
Obj.	Him	Her	It.
	Deuce	a	bit!

CASE.	PLURAL.
Nom.	They
Poss.	Theirs.
Obj.	Them.

Reader, Mem.

We beg to inform thee, that the third person plural has no distinction of gender.

SECTION II.
OF THE RELATIVE PRONOUNS.

The Pronouns called Relative are such as relate, for the most part, to some word or phrase, called the antecedent, on account of its going before: they are, *who*, *which*, and *that*: as, "The man *who* does not drink enough when he can get it, is a fool; but he *that* drinks too much is a beast."

What is usually equivalent to *that which*, and is, therefore, a kind of compound relative, containing both the antecedent and the relative; as, "You want *what* you'll very soon have!" that is to say, *the thing which* you will very soon have.

Who is applied to persons, *which* to animals and things without life; as, "He is a *gentleman who* keeps a horse and lives respectably." "To the *dog which* pinned the old woman, they cried, 'Cæsar!'" "This is the *tree which* Larkins called a *helm*."

Larkins.—I say, Nibbs, ven is a helm box like a asthmatical chest?

Nibbs.—Ven it's a *coffin*.

That, as a relative, is used to prevent the too frequent repetition of *who* and *which*, and is applied both to persons and things; as, "*He that* stops the bottle is a *Cork* man." "This is the house *that* Jack built."

Who is of both numbers; and so is an Editor; for, according to what we observed just now, he is both singular and plural. *Who*, we repeat, is of both numbers, and is thus declined:—

SINGULAR AND PLURAL.

Nominative.   Who

Is the maiden to woo?

Genitive.   Whose

Hand shall I choose?

Accusative.   Whom

To despair shall I doom?

Which, *that*, and *what* are indeclinable; except that *whose* is sometimes used as the possessive case of *which*; as,

> "The roe, poor dear, laments amain,
> *Whose* sweet hart was by hunter slain."

Thus *whose* is substituted for *of which*, in the following example:—

> "There is a blacking famed, *of which*
> The sale made Day and Martin rich;
> There is another blacking, *whose*
> Compounder patronised the Muse."[2]

Who, *which*, and *what*, when they are used in asking questions, are called Interrogatives; as, "*Who* is Mr. Walker?" "*Which* is the left side of a round plum-pudding?" "*What* is the damage?"

Those who have made popular phraseology their study, will have found that *which* is sometimes used for *whereas*, and words of like signification; as in Dean Swift's "Mary the Cookmaid's Letter to Dr. Sheridan":—

---

[2] See Warren's "Ode to Kitty of Shoe Lane," Advertisements, London Press, *passim*.

"And now I know whereby you would fain make an excuse,
Because my master one day in anger call'd you a goose;
Which, and I am sure I have been his servant since October,
And he never called me worse than sweetheart, drunk or sober."

What, or, to speak more *improperly*, *wot*, is generally substituted by cabmen and costermongers for *who*; as, "The donkey *wot* wouldn't go." "The man *wot* sweeps the crossing."

That, likewise, is very frequently rejected by the vulgar, who use *as* in its place; as, "Them *as* asks shan't have any; and them *as* don't ask don't want any."

SECTION III.
OF THE ADJECTIVE PRONOUNS.

Adjective pronouns partake of the nature of both pronouns and adjectives. They may be subdivided into four sorts: the possessive, the distributive, the demonstrative, and the indefinite.

The possessive pronouns are those which imply possession or property. Of these there are seven; namely, *my, thy, his, her, our, your, their*.

The word *self* is added to possessives; as, myself, yourself, "Says I to myself, says I." *Self* is also sometimes used with personal pronouns; as, himself, itself, themselves. *His* self is a common, but not a proper expression.

SELF-ESTEEM

The distributive are three: *each, every, either*; they denote the individual persons or things separately, which, when taken together, make up a number.

Each is used when two or more persons or things are mentioned singly; as, "*each* of the Catos;" "*each* of the Browns."

Every relates to one out of several; as, "*Every* mare is a horse, but *every* horse is not a mare."

Either refers to one out of two; as,

> "When I between two jockeys ride,
> I have a knave on *either* side."

Neither signifies "not either;" as "*Neither* of the Bacons was related to Hogg."

The demonstrative pronouns precisely point out the subjects to which they relate; such are *this* and *that*, with their plurals *these* and *those*; as, "*This* is a foreign Prince; *that* is an English Peer."

This refers to the nearest person or thing, and to the latter or last mentioned; *that* to the most distant, and to the former or first mentioned; as, "*This* is a man; *that* is a nondescript." "At the period of the Reformation in Scotland, a curious contrast between the ancient and modern ecclesiastical systems was observed; for while *that* had been always maintained by a *Bull*, *this* was now supported by a *Knox*."

The indefinite are those which express their subjects in an indefinite or general manner; as, *some, other, any, one, all, such*, &c.

When the definite article *the* comes before the word *other*, those who do not know better, are accustomed to strike out the *he* in *the*, and to say, *t'other*.

The same persons also use *other* in the comparative degree; for sometimes, instead of saying quite the reverse, or perhaps re*w*erse, they avail themselves of the expression, *more t'other*.

So much for the Pronouns.

CHAPTER VI.

OF VERBS.

SECTION I.
OF THE NATURE OF VERBS IN GENERAL.

The nature of Verbs in general, and that in all languages, is, that they are the most difficult things in the Grammar.

Verbs are divided into Active, Passive, and Neuter; and also into Regular, Irregular, and Defective. To these divisions we beg to add another; Verbs Comic.

A Verb Active implies an agent, and an object acted upon; as, to love; "I love Wilhelmina Stubbs." Here, I am the agent; that is, the lover; and Wilhelmina Stubbs is the object acted upon, or the beloved object.

"FACT, MADAM!" "GRACIOUS, MAJOR!"

A Verb Passive expresses the suffering, feeling, or undergoing of something; and therefore implies an object acted upon, and an agent by which it is acted upon; as, to be loved; "Wilhelmina Stubbs is loved by me."

A Verb Neuter expresses neither action nor passion, but a state of being; as, I bounce, I lie.

Of Verbs Regular, Irregular, and Defective, we shall have somewhat to say hereafter.

Verbs Comic are, for the most part, verbs which cannot be found in the dictionary, and are used to express ordinary actions in a jocular manner; as, to "morris," to "bolt," to "mizzle," which signify to go or to depart; to "bone," to "prig," that is to say, to steal; to "collar," which means to seize, an expression probably derived from the mode of prehension, or rather apprehension characteristic of the New Police, as it is one very much in the mouths of those who most frequently come in contact with that body: to "lush," or drink; to "grub," or eat; to "sell," or deceive, &c.

Under the head of Verbs Comic, the Yankee-isms, I "calculate," I "reckon," I "realise," I "guess," and the like, may also be properly enumerated.

Auxiliary, or helping Verbs (by the way, we marvel that the Americans do not call their servants auxiliaries instead of helps,) are those, by the help of which we are chiefly enabled to conjugate our verbs in English. They are, do, be, have, shall, will, may, can, with their variations; and let and must, which have no variation.

Let, however, when it is *anything but* a *helping* verb, as, for instance, when it signifies to *hinder*, makes lettest and letteth. The phrase, "This House to Let," generally used instead of "to be let," really meaning the reverse of what it is intended to convey, is a piece of comic English.

To verbs belong Number, Person, Mood, and Tense. These may be called the properties of a verb; and like those of opium, they are soporiferous properties. There are two very important objects which the writer of every book has, or ought to have in view, to get a reader who is wide awake, and to keep him so:—the latter of which, when Number, Person, Mood, and Tense are to be treated of, is no such easy matter; seeing that the said writer is then in some danger of going to sleep himself. Never mind. If we nod, let the reader wink. What can't be cured must be endured.

SECTION II.
OF NUMBER AND PERSON.

Verbs have two numbers, the Singular and the Plural; as, "I fiddle, we fiddle," &c.

In each number there are three persons; as

	SINGULAR.	PLURAL.
First Person	I love	We love.

Second Person	Thou lovest	Ye or you love.
Third Person	He loves	They love.

What a deal there is in every Grammar about love! Here the following Lines, by a Young Lady (now no more), addressed to Lindley Murray, deserve to be recorded:—

> "Oh, Murray! fatal name to me,
> Thy burning page with tears is wet;
> Since first 'to love' I learned of thee,
> Teach me, ah! teach me 'to forget!'"

SECTION III.
OF MOODS AND PARTICIPLES.

Mood or Mode is a particular form of the verb, or a certain variation which it undergoes, showing the manner in which the being, action, or passion, is represented.

The moods of verbs are five, the Indicative, the Imperative, the Potential, the Subjunctive, and the Infinitive.

The Indicative Mood simply points out or declares a thing: as, "He teaches, he is taught;" or it asks a question: as, "Does he teach? Is he taught?"

Q. Why is old age the best teacher?

A. Because he gives you the most *wrinkles*.

Q. Why does a rope support a rope-dancer?

A. Because it is *taught*.

The Imperative Mood commands, exhorts, entreats, or permits: as, "Vanish thou; trot ye; let us hop; be off!"

The Potential Mood implies possibility or liberty, power, will, or obligation: as, "A waiter *may be* honest. You may stand upon truth or lie. I can filch. He would cozen. They should learn."

The Subjunctive Mood is used to represent a thing as done conditionally; and is preceded by a conjunction, expressed or understood, and accompanied by another verb: as, "*If* the skies should fall, larks would be caught." "Were I to punch your head, I should serve you right;" that is, "*if* I were to punch your head."

The Infinitive Mood expresses a thing generally, without limitation, and without any distinction of number or person: as, "to quarrel, to fight, to be licked."

The Participle is a peculiar form of the verb, and is so called, because it participates in the properties both of a verb and of an adjective: as, "May I have the pleasure of *dancing* with you?" "*Mounted* on a tub he addressed the bystanders." "*Having* uplifted a stave, they departed."

The Participles are three; the Present or Active, the Perfect or Passive, and the Compound Perfect: as, "I felt nervous at the thought of *popping* the question, but that once *popped*, I was not sorry for *having popped* it."

The worst of *popping* the question is, that the *report* is always sure to get abroad.

SECTION IV.
OF THE TENSES.

Tense is the distinction of time, and consists of six divisions, namely, the Present, the Imperfect, the Perfect, the Pluperfect, and the First and Second Future Tenses.

Time is also distinguished by a fore lock, scythe, and hour-glass; but the youthful reader must bear in mind, that these things are not to be confounded with tenses.

The Present Tense, as its name implies, represents an action or event occurring at the present time: as, "I lament; rogues prosper; the mob rules."

The Imperfect Tense represents a past action or event, but which, like a mutton chop, may be either thoroughly done, or not thoroughly done; were it *meet*, we should say *under-done*: as,

> "When I *was* a little boy some fifteen years ago,
> My mammy *doted* on me—Lork! she *made* me quite a show."

> "When our reporter left, the Honourable Gentleman *was* still
> on his legs."

The legs of most "Honourable Gentlemen" must be tolerably stout ones; for the "majority" do not stand on trifles. However, we are not going to *commit* ourselves, like *some* folks, nor to get *committed*, like *other* folks; so we will leave "*Honourable* Gentlemen" to manage matters their own way.

The Perfect Tense declares a thing to have been done at some time, though an indefinite one, antecedent to the present time. That, however, which the Perfect Tense represents as done, is completely, or, as we say of John Bull, when he is humbugged by the thimble-rig people, regularly done; as, "I *have been* out on the river." "I *have caught* a crab."

Catching a crab is a thing *regularly* (in another sense than completely) done, when civic swains pull young ladies up to Richmond. We beg to inform persons unacquainted with aquatic phraseology, that "pulling up" young ladies, or others, is a very different thing from "pulling up" an omnibus conductor or a cabman. What an equivocal language is ours! How much less agreeable to be "pulled up" at Bow Street than to be "pulled up" in a wherry! how wide the discrepancy between "pulling up" radishes and "pulling up" horses!

The Pluperfect Tense represents a thing as doubly past; that is, as past previously to some other point of time also past; as, "I fell in love before I *had arrived* at years of discretion."

The First Future Tense represents the action as yet to come, either at a certain or an uncertain time; as, "The tailor *will send* my coat home to-morrow; and when

I find it perfectly convenient, I *shall pay* him."

YEARS OF DISCRETION

The Second Future intimates that the action will be completed at or before the time of another future action or event; as, "I wonder how many conquests I *shall have made* by to-morrow morning."

N.B. One ball is often the means of killing a great many people.

The consideration of the tenses suggests various moral reflections to the thinking mind.

A few examples will perhaps suffice:—

1. *Present*, though moderate fruition, is preferable to splendid, but contingent *futurity*; i. e. A bird in the hand is worth two in the bush.

2. *Imperfect* nutrition is less to be deprecated than privation of aliment;—a new way of putting an old proverb, which we need not again insert, respecting half a loaf.

3. *Perfect* callidity was the distinguishing attribute of the Curved Pedestrian.

Callidity is another word for craftiness; but for the exercise of the reader's ingenuity, we forbear to mention the person alluded to as so remarkable for his astutious qualities.

Q. What species of *writing* is most conducive to morality?

A. *Text*-hand.

SECTION V.
THE CONJUGATION OF THE AUXILIARY VERBS TO HAVE AND TO BE.

We have observed that boys, in conjugating verbs, give no indications of delight, except that which an ingenuous disposition always feels in the acquisition of knowledge. Now, having arrived at that part of the Grammar in which it becomes necessary that these same verbs should be considered, we feel ourselves in an awkward dilemma. The omission of the conjugations is a *serious* omission—which, of course, is objectionable in a *comic* work—and the insertion of them would be equally serious, and therefore quite as improper. What *shall* we do? We will adopt a middle course; referring the reader to Murray and other talented authors for full information on these matters; and requesting him to be content with our confining ourselves to what is more especially suitable to these pages—a short summary of the *Comicalities* of verbs.

The Conjugation of a verb is the combination and arrangement of its numbers, persons, moods, and tenses.

The Comicalities of verbs consist in certain liberties taken with their numbers, persons, moods, and tenses.

The Conjugation of an active verb is called the Active Voice, and that of a passive Verb the Passive Voice.

If verbs have voices, it is but reasonable that walls should have ears.

The auxiliary and active verb To Have is thus peculiarly conjugated by some people in some of its moods and tenses.

TO HAVE.

INDICATIVE MOOD.

PRESENT TENSE.

SINGULAR.	PLURAL.
1. Pers. I has.	1. Pers. We has.
2. Thee'st.	2. Ye or you has.
3. He've.	3. They has.

PERFECT TENSE.

SINGULAR.	PLURAL.
1. I'ze had.	1. We'ze had.
2. Thee'st had.	2. Ye or you'ze had.
3. He've had.	3. They'ze had.

FIRST FUTURE TENSE

SINGULAR.	PLURAL.
1. I sholl *or* ool ha'.	1. We shool *or* ool ha'.
2. Thee shat *or* oot ha'.	2. Ye or you sholl *or* ool ha'.
3. He sholl *or* ool ha'.	3. They sholl *or* ool ha'.

IMPERATIVE MOOD

SINGULAR.	PLURAL.
1. Let me ha'.	1. Let's ha'.
2. Ha', *or* ha thou, *or* do thee ha'.	2. Ha, *or* ha ye, *or* do ye, *or* you ha'.
3. Let un ha'.	3. Let um ha'.

POTENTIAL MOOD.

PRESENT TENSE

SINGULAR.	PLURAL.
1. I med *or* can ha'.	1. We med *or* can ha'.
2. Thee medst *or* canst ha'.	2. Ye *or* you med *or* can ha'.
3. He med *or* can ha'.	3. They med *or* can ha'.

SUBJUNCTIVE MOOD.

PRESENT TENSE.

SINGULAR.	PLURAL.
1. If I has.	1. If we has.
2. If thee hast	2. If ye or you has.
3. If he ha'.	3. If they has.

INFINITIVE MOOD.

Present, To ha'.	Perfect, To a had.

PARTICIPLES.

Present or Active,	Havun or Avun.
Perfect,	'Ad.
Compound Perfect,	Havun 'ad.

The auxiliary and neuter verb To Be, is maltreated as follows:

TO BE.

(Toby or not Toby? — that is the question!)

INDICATIVE MOOD.

PRESENT TENSE.

SINGULAR.	PLURAL.

1. I be.	1. We be.
2. Thee bist.	2. Ye *or* you be.
3. He, she or it am.	3. They be *or* am.

IMPERFECT TENSE.

SINGULAR.	PLURAL.
1. I wor, or wus.	1. We wus.
2. Thee wort.	2. Ye *or* you wus.
3. He wur.	3. They wur.

"When I say as you was, I mean, as you were."

PERFECT TENSE.

SINGULAR.	PLURAL.
1. I've a bin.	1. We've a bin.
2. Thee'st a bin.	2. Ye *or* you've a bin.
3. He've a bin.	3. They've a bin.

IMPERATIVE MOOD.

SINGULAR.	PLURAL.
1. Let I be.	1. Let we be.
2. Be thee *or* 'st thee be.	2. Do 'ee be.
3. Let un be.	3. Let um be.

INFINITIVE MOOD.

Present Tense, For to be.	Perfect, For to ha' bin.

PARTICIPLES.

Present, Beun.	Perfect, Bin.
Compound Perfect,	Havun bin.

If *being* a younster, I had not been smitten,
Of *having been* jilted I should not complain,
Take warning from me all ye lads who are bitten,
When this part of Grammar occurs to your brain.

As there is a certain *intensity* of feeling abroad, which renders people indisposed to trouble themselves with *verbal* matters, we shall take the liberty of making very short work of the Regular Verbs. Even Murray can only afford to conjugate one example,—To Love. The learner must amplify this part of the Grammar for himself: and we recommend him to substitute for "to love," some word less harrowing to a sensitive mind: as, "to fleece, to tax," verbs which excite disagreeable emotions only in a sordid one; and which also, by association of ideas, conduct us to useful reflections on Political Economy. We advise all whom it may concern, however, to pay the greatest attention to this part of the Grammar, and before they come to the Verbs Regular, to make a particular study of the Auxiliary Verbs: not only for the excellent reasons set forth in "Tristram Shandy," but also to avoid those awkward mistakes in which the Comicalities of the Verbs, or Verbal Comicalities, chiefly consist.

"Did it rain to-morrow?" asked Monsieur Grenouille.

"Yes it was!" replied Monsieur Crapaud.

We propose the following as an *auxiliary mode* of conjugating verbs:—"I love to roam on the crested foam, Thou lovest to roam on the crested foam, He loves to roam on the crested foam, We love to roam on the crested foam, Ye or you love to roam on the crested foam, They love to roam on the crested foam," &c. These words, if set to music, might serve for a grammatical *glee*, and would, at all events, be productive of *mirth*.

"I SHALL GIVE YOU A DRUBBING!"

The Auxiliary Verbs, too, are very useful when a peculiar emphasis is required: as, "I shall give you a drubbing!" "*Will* you?" "I know a trick worth two of that." "*Do* you, though?" "It *might*," as the Quaker said to the Yankee, who wanted to know what his name might be; "it *might* be Beelzebub, but it *is* not."

Now we may as well say what we have to say about the conjugation of regular verbs active.

SECTION VI.
THE CONJUGATION OF REGULAR VERBS ACTIVE.

Regular Verbs Active are known by their forming their imperfect tense of the indicative mood, and their perfect participle, by adding to the verb *ed*, or *d* only when the verb ends in *e*: as,

PRESENT.	IMPERFECT.	PERF. PARTICIP.
I reckon.	I reckoned.	Reckoned.
I realise.	I realised.	Realised.

Here should follow the conjugation of the regular active verb, or, as a Cockney Romeo would say, the *regular* torturing verb, To Love; but we have already assigned a good reason for omitting it; besides which we have to say, that we think it a verb highly unfit for conjugation by youth, as it tends to put ideas into their heads which they would otherwise never have thought of; and it is moreover our opinion, that several of our most gifted poets may, with reason, have attributed those unfortunate attachments which, though formed in early youth, served to embitter their whole lives, to the poison which they thus sucked in with the milk, so to speak, of their Mother Tongue, the Grammar.

PASSIVE.

Verbs Passive are said to be regular, when their perfect participle is formed by the addition of *d*, or *ed* to the verb: as, from the verb "To bless," is formed the passive, "I am blessed, I was blessed, I shall be blessed," &c.

The conjugation of a passive verb is nothing more than the repetition of that of the auxiliary To Be, the perfect participle being added.

And now, having cut the regular verbs (as Alexander did the Gordian knot) instead of conjugating them, let us proceed to consider the

IRREGULAR VERBS.

SECTION VII.
IRREGULAR VERBS.

Irregular Verbs are those of which the imperfect tense and the perfect participle are *not* formed by adding *d* or *ed* to the verb: as,

PRESENT.	IMPERFECT.	PERFECT PART.
I blow.	I blew.	blown.

To say I am blown, is, under certain circumstances, such as windy and tempestuous weather, proper enough; but I am blowed, it will at once be perceived, is not only an ungrammatical, but also a vulgar expression.

Great liberties are taken with the Irregular Verbs, insomuch that in the mouths of some persons, divers of them become doubly irregular in the formation of their participles. Among such Irregular Verbs we may enumerate the following:—

PRESENT.	IMPERFECT.	PERF. OR PASS. PART.
Am	wur	bin.
Beat	bet *or* bate	bate.
Burst	bust	busted.
Catch	cotch	cotched
Come	kim	comed.
Creep	crup	crup.
Drive	druv	driv.
Freeze	friz	froze.
Give	guv	giv.
Go	goed	went.
Rise	riz	rose.
See	sid	sin, &c.

Some verbs which in this country are held to be regular, are treated as irregular verbs in America: as,

PRESENT.	IMPERFECT.	PERF. OR PASS. PART.
Row	rew	rown.
Snow	snew	snown.

SECTION VIII.
OF DEFECTIVE VERBS.

Most men have five senses,
Most verbs have six tenses;
But as there are some folks
Who are blind, deaf, or dumb folks,
Just so there are some verbs
Defective, or *rum* verbs,

which are used only in some of their moods and tenses.

The principal of them are these:—

	IMPERF.	PERF. OR PASS. PART.
Can	could	nix.
May	might	—
Shall	should	—

Will	would	—
Must	must	—
Ought	ought	—
—	quoth	—

There is not, perhaps, anything in the defective verbs peculiarly valuable in a comic point of view. However, it should not be forgotten, that

Can is one of the signs of the POT-ential Mood;

Will, Would reminds us of the Drapier's Letters.

"Must" is for the House of Commons (it used to be for the King).

Ought, ought, with 1 before it, stands, (in schoolboy phrase) for 100.

'Tis naught, so to speak, however, says Murray.

CHAPTER VII.
OF ADVERBS.

Having as great a dislike as the youngest of our readers can have to repetitions, we shall not say what an adverb is over again. It is, nevertheless, right to observe, that some adverbs are compared: as, far, farther, farthest; near, nearer, nearest. In comparing those which end in *ly*, we use *more* and *most*: as, slowly, more slowly, most slowly.

Q. Who, of all the civic functionaries, moves "most slowly?"

A. Mr. Hobler.

There are a great many adverbs in the English Language: their number is probably even greater than that of abusive epithets. They are divisible into certain classes; the chief of which are Number, Order, Place, Time, Quantity, Manner or Quality, Doubt, Affirmation, Negation, Interrogation, and Comparison.

A nice little list, truly! and perhaps some of our readers may suppose that we are going to exemplify it at length: if so, all we can say with regard to their expectation is, that we wish they may get it gratified. In the meantime, we will not turn our Grammar into a dictionary, to please anybody. However, we have no objection to a brief illustration of the uses and properties of adverbs, as contained in the following passage:—

"*Formerly, when first* I began to preach and to teach, *whithersoever* I went, the little boys followed me, and *now* and *then* pelted me with brick-bats, as *heretofore* they pelted Ebenezer Grimes. And *whensoever* I opened my mouth, *straightways* the ungodly began to crow. *Oftentimes* was I hit in the mouth with an orange: *yea*, and *once, moreover*, with a rotten egg; *whereat* there was much laughter, which, *notwithstanding*, I took in good part, and wiped my face, and looked *pleasantly*. For *peradventure* I said, they will listen to my sermon; *yea*, and after that we may have a collection. So I was *nowise* discomfited; *wherefore* I advise thee, Brother Habakkuk, to take no heed of thy persecutors, seeing that I, *whereas* I was once little better off than thyself, have *now* a chapel of mine own. And *herein* let thy mind be comforted, that, preach as much as thou wilt against the Bishop, thou wilt not, *therefore*, in these days, be in danger of the pillory. Howbeit," &c.

Vide Life of the late pious and Rev. Samuel Simcox (letter to Habbakuk Brown).

CHAPTER VIII.

OF PREPOSITIONS.

Prepositions are, for the most part, put before nouns and pronouns: as, "out *of* the frying-pan *into* the fire."

Two prepositions, *with* and *without*, are sometimes (as we have been informed) used in the place of substantives: as, "cold *without,* warm *with.*"

The preposition *of* is sometimes used as a part of speech of peculiar signification, and one to which no name has as yet been applied: as, "What have you been doing *of?*"

At and *up* are not rarely used as verbs, but we should scarcely have been justified in so classing them by the authority of any polite writer; such use of them being confined to the vulgar: as, "Now then, Bill, *at* him again." "So she *upped* with her fists, and fetched him a whop."

After is improperly pronounced *arter,* and *against, agin*: as, "Hallo! Jim, vot are you *arter*? don't you know that ere's *agin* the Law?"

CHAPTER IX.
OF CONJUNCTIONS.

A Conjunction means literally, a union or meeting together. An ill-assorted marriage is

A COMICAL CONJUNCTION

But our conjunctions are used to connect words and sentences, and have nothing to do with the joining of hands. They are chiefly of two sorts, the Copulative and Disjunctive.

The Copulative Conjunction is employed for the connection or continuation of a sentence: as, "Jack *and* Gill went up the Hill," "I will sing a song *if* Gubbins will,"

"A thirsty man is like a City Giant, *because* he is a Gog for drink."

The Conjunction Disjunctive is used not only for purposes of connection, but also to express opposition of meaning in different degrees: as, "*Though* Lord John is as cunning as a Fox, *yet* Sir Robert is as deep as a Pitt." "We pay less for our letters, *but* shall have to pay more for our panes: they have lightened our postage, *but* they will darken our rooms."

Conjunctions are the hooks and eyes of Language, in which, as well as in dress, it is very possible to make an awkward use of them: as, "For *if* the year consist of 365 days 6 hours, *and* January have 31 days, *then* the relation between the corpuscular theory of light *and* the new views of Mr. Owen is at once subverted: *for*, 'When Ignorance is bliss, 'tis folly to be wise:' *because* 1760 yards make a mile; *and* it is universally acknowledged that 'war is the madness of many for the gain of a few:' *therefore* Sir Isaac Newton was quite right in supposing the diamond to be combustible."

The word *as*, so often used in this and other Grammars, is a conjunction: as, "Mrs. A. is *as* well *as* can be expected."

"AS WELL AS CAN BE EXPECTED"

The Siamese twins formed a singular conjunction.

A tin pot fastened to a dog's tail is a disagreeable conjunction to the unfortunate animal.

A happy pair may be regarded as an uncommon conjunction.

CHAPTER X.
INTERJECTIONS.

We have said almost enough about their Etymology already. Still, it may not be superfluous to bestow a passing notice on the singularly expressive character of certain of these parts of speech, heard, it is true, repeatedly; but unaccountably omitted in all previous Grammars. For instance, how many lives does the warning, "Hoy!" of the coachman or cab-driver daily save? What an amount of infantile aberrations from propriety is the admonitory "Paw-paw!" the means of checking. With what felicity is acquiescence denoted by "Umph!" The utility of the Interjections on various occasions, such as our meals, for example, in enabling us to economise our speech, is very striking.

CHAPTER XI.
OF DERIVATION.

Those who know Latin, Greek, Saxon, and the other languages from which our own is formed, do not require to be instructed in philological derivation; and on those who do not understand the said tongues, such instruction would be thrown away. In what manner English words are derived, one from another, the generality of persons know very well: there are, however, a few words and phrases, which it is expedient to trace to their respective sources; not only because such an exercise is of itself delightful to the inquiring mind; but because we shall thereby be furnished (as we hope to show) with a test by means of which, on hearing an expression for the first time, we shall be able, in most instances, to decide at once respecting its nature and quality.

There are several words in the English Language which were originally Terms of Art, but came in process of time to be applied metaphorically to the common purposes of discourse. Thus lodgings are sometimes called *quarters*; a word which, in its restricted sense, signifies the lodgings of soldiers; ill habits, like diseases, are said to be *remedied*; men hope, as if indicted for an offence, that ladies will *acquit* them of inattention, and so forth. When, as in the instances cited, the word or phrase can be traced back either to one of the Learned Professions, or to any source savouring of gentility, it is esteemed a proper one, and there is no objection to its use.

Now we have divers other words, of which many have but recently come into vogue, which, though by no means improper or immoral, are absolutely unutterable in any polite assembly. It is not, at first, very easy to see what can be the objection to their use; but derivation explains it for us in the most satisfactory manner. The truth is, that the expressions in question take their origin from various trades and occupations, in which they have, for the most part, a literal meaning; and we now perceive what horrible suspicions respecting one's birth, habits, and education, their figurative employment would be likely to excite. To make the matter indisputably clear, we will explain our position by a few examples.

WORDS AND PHRASES.	WHAT DERIVED FROM.
Bone (to steal),	Butchers.
Chisel (to cheat),	Carpenters.
Clout (to beat),	Scullions.
To cut it fat,	Cooks.

To come it strong,	Publicans.
To draw it mild,	Ditto.
To drop off the hooks,	Butchers.
To miss your tip,	Footmen.
To be done,	Cooks.
To be done brown,	Ditto.
To collar (to seize),	Thieves or policemen.
To be walked off,	Ditto.
A sell,	Jews.
A shine,	Shoe-boys.
A wipe (a handkerchief),	Blackguards in general, from its use.
A mawley (a hand),	Prizefighters.
To welt (to beat),	Cobblers.
To leather (ditto),	Ditto.
To strap (ditto),	Ditto.
To hide (ditto),	Curriers.
Spicy (showy),	Grocers.
To hang out (to dwell),	Publicans.
A drag (carriage),	Stage-coachmen.
Swamped (ruined),	Watermen.
To put one's oar in (to interfere),	Watermen.
Get on with your barrow,	Dogs'-meat-men.
Kidderminster (for carpet),	Upholsterers.
Mahogany (for table),	Ditto.
Dodge (trick),	Pickpockets.

(N.B. All those are obliged to have recourse to the *dodge*, who are in the habit of *outrunning* the constable.) But, to proceed with our Etymology:

To bung up an eye,	Brewers.
To chalk down,	Publicans.
A close shaver (a miser),	Barbers.
To be off your feed,	Ostlers.
Hold hard (stop),	Omnibus-men.

Numerous examples, similar to the foregoing, will, no doubt, present themselves, in addition, to the mind of the enlightened student. We have not, however, quite done yet with our remarks on this division of our subject. The intrinsic vulgarity of all modes of speech which may be traced to mean or disreputable persons, will, of course, not be questioned. But—and as we have got hold of a nice bone, we may as well get all the marrow we can out of it—the principle which is now under consideration has a much wider range than is apparent at first sight.

Now we will suppose a red-hot lover addressing the goddess of his idolatry—by the way, how strange it is, that these goddesses should be always having their temples on fire, that a Queen of Hearts should ever be seated on a burning throne!—but to return to the lover: he was to say something. Well, then, let A. B. be the lover. He expresses himself thus:—

"Mary, my earthly hopes are centred in you. You need not doubt me; my heart is true as the dial to the sun. Words cannot express how much I love you. Nor is my affection an ordinary feeling: it is a more exalted and a more enduring sentiment than that which usually bears its name. I have done. I am not eloquent: I can say no more, than that I deeply and sincerely love you."

This, perhaps, will be regarded by connoisseurs as tolerably pathetic, and for the kind of thing not very ridiculous. Now, let A. S. S. be the lover; and let us have his version of the same story:—

"Mary, my capital in life is invested in you. You need not stick at giving me credit; my heart is as safe as the Bank of England. The sum total of my love for you defies calculation. Nor is my attachment anything in the common way. It is a superior and more durable article than that in general wear. My stock of words is exhausted. I am no wholesale dealer in that line. All I can say is, that I have a vast fund of unadulterated affection for you."

In this effusion the Stock Exchange, the Multiplication Table, and the Linendraper's and Grocer's shops have been drawn upon for a clothing to the suitor's ideas; and by an unhappy choice of words, the most delightful and amiable feelings of our nature, without which Life would be a Desert and Man a bear, are invested with a ridiculous disguise.

We would willingly enlarge upon the topic which we have thus slightly handled, but that we feel that we should by so doing, intrench too far on the boundaries of Rhetoric, to which science, more particularly than to Grammar, the consideration of Metaphor belongs; besides which, it is high time to have done with Etymology. Here, then, gentlemen, if you please, we shall pull up.

"Pull up! what an expression!"

"Well, Sir, did you never hear that next to the *Bar* the first school of grammatical elegance is the *Stage*?"

PART III.
SYNTAX.

SYNTAX.

"Now then, reader, if you are quite ready, we are—All right! * * * *"

The asterisks are intended to stand for a word used in speaking to horses. Don't blush, young ladies; there's not a shadow of harm in it: but as to spelling it, we are as unable to do so as the ostler's boy was, who was thrashed for his ignorance by his father.

"Where are we now, coachman?"

SYNTAX.

"The third part of Grammar, Sir, wot treats of the agreement and construction of words in a sentence."

"Does a coachman say *wot* for *which* because he has a licence?"

"Can't say, Ma'am?"

"Drive on, coachman."

And *we* must *drive on*, or *boil on*, or whatever it is the fashion to call getting on in these times.

A sentence is an aggregate of words forming a complete sense.

Sometimes, however, a sentence is an aggregate of words forming complete nonsense: as,

"They are very civil and attentive to the smallest order, and furnish a house entirely complete, *for twenty-seven guineas, all new and well seasoned.*"—Advertisement in the Times.

Sentences are of two kinds, simple and compound.

A simple sentence has in it but one subject and one finite verb; that is, a verb to which number and person belong: as, "A joke is a joke."

A compound sentence consists of two or more simple sentences connected together: as, "A joke is a joke, but a ducking is no joke. Corpulence is the attribute of swine, mayors, and oxen."

Simple sentences may be divided (if we choose to take the trouble) into the Explicative or explaining; the Interrogative, or asking; the Imperative, or commanding.

An explicative sentence is, in other words, a direct assertion: as, "Sir, you are impertinent."—*Johnson.*

An interrogative sentence "merely asks a question:" as, "Are you a policeman? How's your Inspector?"

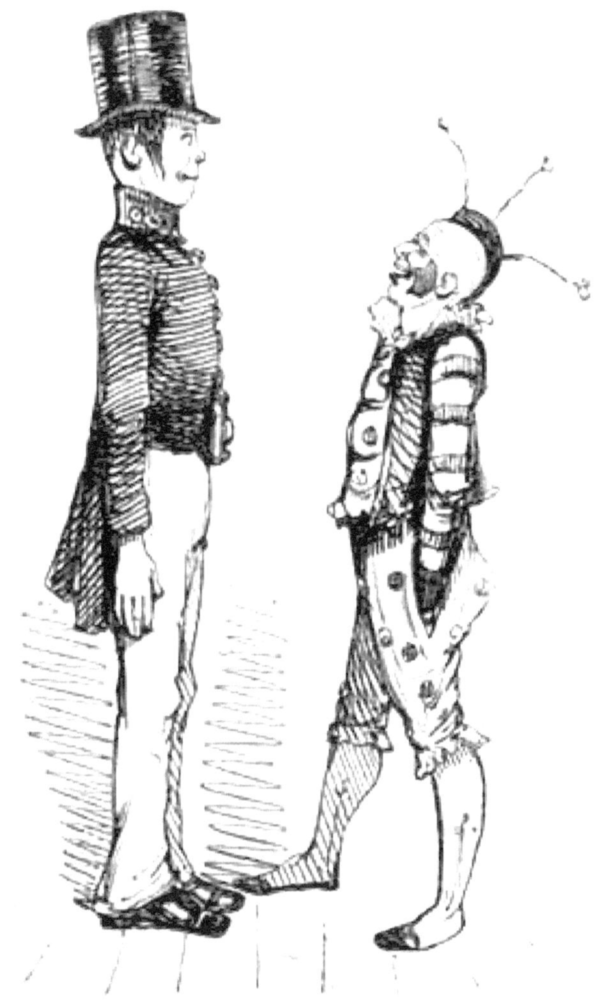

"HOW'S YOUR INSPECTOR?"

An imperative sentence is expressive of command, exhortation, or entreaty: as, "Shoulder arms!" "Turn out your toes!" "Charge bayonets!"

A phrase is two or more words properly put together, making either a sentence or part of a sentence: as, "Good morning!" "Your most obedient!"

Some phrases consist of two or more words improperly put together: these are improper phrases: as, "Now then, old stupid!" "Stand out of the sunshine!"

Other phrases consist of words put together by ladies: as, "A duck of a man," "A love of a shawl," "*so* nice," "quite refreshing," "sweetly pretty." "Did you ever?" "No I never!"

"WHAT A DUCK OF A MAN!"

Other phrases again consist of French and English words put together by people of quality, because their knowledge of both languages is pretty nearly equal: as, "I am au désespoir," "mis hors de combat," "quite ennuyé," or rather in nine cases out of ten, "ennuyée," — "I have a great envie" to do so and so. These constitute an important variety of comic English.

Besides the above, there are various phrases which we may call elliptical phrases, consisting principally of the peculiar terms employed in the different trades and professions: as,

"A Milton Lost," by booksellers.

"A Lady (of the Lake) in sheets," do.

"One college (pudding) for No. 6," by waiters.

"To carry off:" as, "See how the old woman in a red cloak carries off the tower," by painters, &c.

The principal parts of a simple sentence are, the subject, the attribute, and the object.

If you want to know what *subjects* and *objects* are, you should go to the Morgue at Paris. But in Grammar—

The subject is the thing chiefly spoken of; the attribute is that which is affirmed or denied of it; and the object is the thing affected by such action.

The nominative denotes the subject, and usually goes before the verb or attribute; and the word or phrase, denoting the object, follows the verb; as, "The flirt torments her lover." Here, *a flirt* is the subject; *torments*, the attribute or thing affirmed; and *her lover*, the object.

THE FLIRT

Yes, and a pretty *object* he is too, sometimes. But then we shall be told that he is *not* an object—of attachment. Alas! that is the very reason why he *is* an object—of compassion, or ridicule, according to people's dispositions.

It may be also said that the flirt herself is a *pretty* object. All we can say is, that we never saw such a flirt, nor do we believe that we ever shall.

To torment, it seems, is the *attribute* of the flirt, as it is that of the — —. Well! no matter. Much good may the fellowship do her: that is all!

It strikes us, though, that we are somewhat digressing from our subject, namely Syntax, which,

Principally consists of two parts (which the flirt does not, for she is all body and no soul) Concord and Government.

Concord is the agreement which one word has with another, in gender, number, case or person.

Note.—That a want of agreement between words does not invalidate *deeds*. We apprehend that such an engagement as the following, properly authenticated, would hold good in law.

> I ose Jon stubs too Poun for valley reseved an promis to pay
> Him Nex Sattaday
>
>   Signed Willum Gibs is >< Mark
>
> March 18, 1840.

Also that a friend of ours, to whom the following bill was sent, could not have refused to discharge it on the score of its incorrect grammar.

1835			Mr. — —			
Jenery 10				To J. Burton.		
				l.	*s.*	*d.*
Reparing of Towo Tables & Muex Stand				0	4	0
Aultern of 2 Blines & Toulroler				0	1	0
Botal jock braket & seter jobs (*et cetera*)				0	4	0
Newpot board Barers & scirtin &c. stapel				0	5	0
Locks to Cubard dowrs & Esing do laying down flour cloth & fiting up Top of Butt				0	7	0
Fixing Lether to Dowrs in parlor & Cuting of sheters in first flour				0	4	0
1 Blin 2 par of Roler End & Rack puleys fixing of certin Laths in Largin of ole of washing stand & 2 holefass				0	2	10
Fixing webbin to Stand and fixing Legs to washing stule				0	1	6
Fiting up front of Dustbin & Cubbard on Landing altern lock of seler dowr				0	2	0
				1	11	4

Government is that power which one part of speech has over another, in directing its mood, tense, or case.

Government is also that power, of which, if the Chartists have their way, we shall soon see very little in this country.

Hurrah!
No taxes!
No army!
No navy!
No parsons!
No lawyers!
No Commons!
No Lords!
No anything!
No nothing!

To produce the agreement and right disposition of words in a sentence, the following rules (and observations?) should be carefully studied.

RULE I.

A verb must agree with its nominative case in number and person: as, "I perceive." "Thou hast been to Brixton." "Apes chatter." "Frenchmen gabble."

Certain liberties are sometimes taken with this rule: as, "I own I likes good beer." "You'm a fine fellow, aint yer?" "He've been to the Squire's." Such modes of speaking are adopted by those who neither know nor care anything about grammatical correctness: but there are other persons who *care* a great deal about it, but unfortunately do not *know* what it consists in. Such folks are very fond of saying, "How it rain!" "It fit you very well." "He say he think it very unbecoming," "I were gone before you was come," and so forth, in which forms of speech they perceive a peculiar elegance.

The infinitive mood, or part of a sentence, is sometimes used as the nominative case to the verb: as "to be good is to be happy:" which is as grammatical an assertion as "Toby Good is Toby Happy;" and rather surpasses it in respect of sense. "That two pippins are a pair, is a proposition which no man in his senses will deny."

"To be a connoisseur in boots,
To hate all rational pursuits,
To make your money fly, as though
Gold would as fast as mushrooms grow;
To haunt the Opera, save whene'er
There's anything worth hearing there;
To smirk, to smile, to bow, to dance,
To talk of what they eat in France,
To languish, simper, sue, and sigh,
And stuff her head with flattery;
Are means to gain that worthless part
A fashionable lady's heart."

Here are examples enough, in all conscience, of infinitive moods serving as nominative cases.

All verbs, save only in the infinitive mood or participle, require a nominative case either expressed or understood: as, "Row with me down the river," that is "Row thou, or do thou row." "Come where the aspens quiver," "come thou, or do thou come." "Fly not yet;" "fly not thou, or do not thou fly." "Pass the ruby;" "pass thou, or do thou pass the ruby" (not the Rubi*con*). "Drink to me only;" "drink thou, or do thou drink only." "Wake, dearest, wake;" "wake thou, or do thou wake." "Tell her I love her;" "tell thou, or do thou tell her I love her." In short, you cannot listen to a hawker of ballads, crying his commodities about the streets, without hearing illustrations of the foregoing rule. "Move on!" the well known mandate of policemen to those who create obstructions, is a very common exemplification of it. The nominative case is easily *understood* in the latter instance; and the person addressed, if he pretend that it is not, does so at his own peril.

A well known popular song affords an example of the violation of this rule.

> "Ven as the Captain comed for to hear on't,
> Wery much applauded vot she'd done."

THE CAPTAIN

The verb applauded has here no nominative case, whereas it ought to have been governed by the pronoun *he*. "He very much applauded," &c.

Every nominative case, except when made absolute, or used, like the Latin Vocative, in addressing a person, should belong to some verb, implied if not expressed. A beautiful example of this grammatical maxim, and one, too, that explains itself, is impressed upon the mind very soon after its first introduction to *letters*: as,

"Who kill'd Cock Robin?
I, said the sparrow,
With my bow and arrow;
I kill'd Cock Robin."

Of the neglect of this rule also, the ballad lately mentioned presents an instance: as,

"Four-and-twenty brisk young fellows
Clad in jackets, blue array,—
And they took poor Billy Taylor
From his true love all avay."

The only verb in these four lines is the verb *took*, which is governed by the pronoun *they*. The four-and-twenty brisk young fellows, therefore, though undeniably in the nominative, have no verb to belong to: while, at the same time, whatever may be thought of their behaviour to Mr. William Taylor, they are certainly not *absolute* in point of case.

When a verb comes between two nouns, either of which may be taken as the subject of the affirmation, it may agree with either of them: as, "Two-and-sixpence *is* half-a-crown." Due regard, however, should be paid to that noun which is most naturally the subject of the verb: it would be clearly wrong to say, "Ducks and green peas *is* a delicacy." "Fleas *is* a nuisance."

A nominative case, standing without a personal tense of a verb, and being put before a participle, independently of the rest of the sentence, is called a case absolute: as, "My brethren, *to-morrow being* Sunday, I shall preach a sermon in Smithfield; after which we shall join in a hymn, *and that having been sung*, Brother Biggs will address you."

The objective case is sometimes incorrectly made absolute by showmen and others: as, "Here, gentlemen and ladies, you will see that great warrior Napoleon Bonaparte, standing agin a tree with his hands in his pockets, *him* taking good care to keep out of harm's vay. And there, on the extreme right, you will observe the Duky Vellinton a valking about amidst the red-hot cannon balls, *him* not caring von straw."

RULE II.

Two or more singular nouns, joined together by a copulative conjunction, expressed or understood, are equivalent to a plural noun, and therefore require verbs, nouns, and pronouns, agreeing with them in the plural number: as, "Veal, wine, and vinegar" (take care how you pronounce these words) "are very good victuals I vow." "Burke and Hare were nice men." "A hat without a crown, a tattered coat, threadbare and out at elbows, a pair of breeches which looked like a piece of dirty patchwork diversified by various holes, and of boots which a Jew would hardly have raked from a kennel, at once proclaimed him a man who had seen better days."

THE DUKE OF WELLINGTON

This rule is not always adhered to in discourse quite so closely as a fastidious ear would require it to be: as, "And so, you know, Mary, and I, and Jane *was* a dusting the chairs, and in comes Missus."

RULE III.

When the conjunction disjunctive comes between two nouns, the verb, noun, or pronoun, is of the singular number, because it refers to each of such nouns taken separately: as, "A cold in the head, or a sore eye *is* a great disadvantage to a lover."

If singular pronouns, or a noun and pronoun of different persons, be disjunctively connected, the verb must agree with the person which stands nearest to it: as "I or thou *art*." "Thou or I *am*." "I, thou, or he *is*," &c. But as this way of writing or speaking is very inelegant, and as saying, "Either I am, or thou art," and so on, will always render having recourse to it unnecessary, the rule just laid down is almost useless, except inasmuch as it suggests a moral maxim, namely, "Always be on good terms with your next door neighbour."

It also forcibly reminds us of some beautiful lines by Moore, in which the heart, like a tendril, is said to twine round the "nearest and loveliest thing." Now the person which is placed nearest the verb is the object of choice; *ergo*, the most agreeable person—*ergo*, the loveliest person or thing.

Should a conjunction disjunctive occur between a singular noun or pronoun, and a plural one, the verb agrees with the plural noun or pronoun: as, "Neither a king nor his courtiers are averse to butter:" (particularly when thickly spread). "Darius or the Persians were hostile to Greece."

RULE IV.

A noun of multitude, that is, one which signifies many, can have a verb or pronoun to agree with it either in the singular or plural number; according to the import of such noun, as conveying unity or plurality of idea: as, "The Parliament *is*—" we do not choose to say what. "The nation *is* humbugged." "The ministry *are* exceedingly well pensioned." "The multitude *have* to pay many taxes." "The Council *are* at a loss to know what to do." "The people *is* a many-headed monster."

We do not mean to call the people names. We only quote what all parties say of it when out of office. When they are *in*, it is—why, we may exhaust the alphabet about it, as Sterne tried to do about Love; but he couldn't get farther than R.; and therefore, if we break down, it is no matter. So we will e'en try a leap; and as the maxim "audi alteram partem" is a favourite one with all rightly constituted minds, our own inclusive, we will see what can be said on both sides. The people, then, is termed,

By the *Ins*.	By the *Outs*.
An apprehensive people,	An addle-headed people.
A blessed people,	A burdened people.
A chivalrous people,	A currish people.
A delightful people,	A disgusting people.
An enlightened people,	An embruted people.
A free people,	A fettered people.
A glorious people,	A grovelling people.
A high-minded people,	A hoggish people.
An intelligent people,	An impenetrable people.
A judicious people,	A jolter-headed people.

A knowing people,	A knotty-pated people.
A lively people,	A lubberly people.
A magnanimous people,	A miserable people.
A noble people,	A niggardly people.
An obliging people,	An odious people.
A pious people,	A profane people.
A quiet people,	A quarrelsome people.
A righteous people,	A rascally people.
A sensible people,	A stupid people.
A Tory people,	A truculent people.
An upright people,	An unprincipled people.
A virtuous people,	A vicious people.
A Whig people,	A wicked people.
An X-cellent people,	An X-ecrable people.
A yielding people,	A yelping people.
A zetetic people,	A zany people.

And now for a little more Syntax.

RULE V.

Pronouns agree with their antecedents, and with the nouns to which they belong, in gender and number: as, "This is the blow *which* killed Ned." "England was once governed by a celebrated King, *who* was called Rufus the Red, but *whose* name was by no means so illustrious as that of Alfred." "His Grace and the Baronet had put on *their* boots." "The Countess appeared, and *she* smiled, but the smile belied *her* feelings."

The relative being of the same person with the antecedent, the verb always agrees with it: as, "Thou *who learnest Syntax*." "I *who enlighten* thy mind."

The relative *what* (incorrectly pronounced) is sometimes used in a manner which is very exceptionable: as, "The gentleman *wot keeps* the wine-vaults." "None but lovers can feel for *them wot loves*." We mention this error once more, in order to insure its abandonment.

The objective case of the personal pronouns is by some, for want of better information, employed in the place of *these* and *those*: as, "Let *them* things alone." "Now then, Jemes, make haste with *them* chops." "Give *them* tables a wipe." "Oh! Julier, turn *them* heyes away." "What's the use o' mancipatin' *them* niggers?" "Don't you wish you was one of *them* lobsters?" "I think *them* shawls *so* pretty!" "Look at *them* sleeves." The adverb *there*, is sometimes, with additional impropriety, joined to the pronoun *them*: as, "Look after *them there* sheep."

The objective case of a pronoun in the first person is put after the interjections

Oh! and *Ah!* as, "Oh! dear me," &c. The second person, however, requires a nominative case: as, "Oh! you good-for-nothing man!" "Ah! thou gay Lothario!"

"OH! YOU GOOD-FOR-NOTHING MAN!"

RULE VI.

When there is no nominative case between the relative and the verb, the relative itself is the nominative to the verb: as, "The master *who* flogged us." "The rods *which* were used."

But when the nominative comes between the relative and the verb, the relative exchanges, as it were, the character of sire for that of son, and becomes the governed instead of the *governor;* depending for its case on some word in its own member of the sentence: as, "He *who* is now at the head of affairs, *whom* the Queen delighteth to honour, *whose* Pavilion (if the Court had been there) might have been at Brighton, and to *whom* is intrusted the helm of state—is a Lamb."

Well, it is to be hoped that he will get on in his boat a little better than a bear; though why that animal is considered so peculiarly *at sea* when on the water, we cannot tell. Man is the only sailor except the nautilus that we know of. Even the steer is no *steersman*. The bear, however, is an ill-conditioned, awkward creature, and very likely to upset the boat; while the more gentle *lamb*, whatever may be the perils of his situation, leaves the rudder alone, remains quietly in his place, and goes with the stream.

RULE VII.

The relative and the verb, when the former is preceded by two nominatives of different persons, may agree in person with either, according to the sense: as, "I am the young gentleman *who do* the lovers at the Wells;" or, "*who does.*"

THE YOUNG GENTLEMAN

Let this maxim be borne constantly in mind. "A *murderer* of good characters should always be made an *example of.*"

RULE VIII.

Every adjective, and every adjective pronoun, relates to a substantive, expressed or implied: as, "Dando was an unprincipled, as well as a voracious man." "Few quarrel with their bread and butter;" that is, "few *persons*." "This is the wonderful eagle of the sun." That is, "This *eagle*," &c.

Adjective pronouns agree in number with their substantives: "This muff, these muffs; that booby, these boobies; another numscull, other numsculls."

Some people say "*Those* kind of things," or, "*This* four-and-twenty year," neither of which expressions they have any business to use.

A good deal of speculation has been expended on the word *means* in connection with an adjective pronoun. Some will have it that we should say, "By this mean;" "By that mean;" "By these means;" "By those means:" others, that we should say, "By *this means*," and so on. The practical rule to be observed is, to treat the substantive, means, as a singular noun when it refers to what is singular, and when it relates to that which is plural, as a plural one. The word *mean* is seldom used in the same sense with means. We have been induced to advert to this question, by the desire of giving the reader a caution respecting the use of this same word, *means*. It is not uncommon to hear it said in the streets and elsewhere, "Well, and then, you know, Jem was took afore the beak, *by means of* which he had three months." "Sall was quite intosticated, by *means* of which (or vich) she wor fined five bob," &c. We will not shock the refined grammarian by the multiplication of examples of this kind; suffice it to say, that the phrase "by means of which" is substituted for "in consequence of which," or, "on which account," by the lower or illiterate classes.

Adjectives are sometimes improperly used as adverbs: as, "He behaved very *bad*." "He insulted me most *gross*." "He eat and drank *uncommon*." "He wur beat very *severe*." "It hailed *tremendous*," or, more commonly, "*tremenjus*."

RULE IX.

The article *a* or *an* agrees with nouns in the singular number only: as, "A fool, an ass, a simpleton, a ninny, a lout—I would not give a farthing for a thousand such."

The definite article *the* may agree with nouns in the singular and plural number: as, "The toast, the ladies, the ducks."

The articles are often properly omitted; when used, they serve to determine or limit the thing spoken of: as, "Variety is charming." "Familiarity doth breed contempt." "*A* stitch in time saves nine." "*The* heart that has truly loved never forgets."

The article *a* or *an* is sometimes (we grieve to say it) applied to nouns in the plural number: as, "A wine-vaults." "An oyster-rooms." But this misapplication of the article is positively shocking.

RULE X.

One substantive, in the possessive or genitive case, is governed by another, of a different meaning: as, "A fiddle-stick's end." "Monkey's allowance." "Virtue's reward."

"VIRTUE'S REWARD"

Pronouns, as well as nouns, are thus governed by substantives: as, "The woes of a kitten (like those of a Poet) are expressed by *its* mews."

RULE XI.

Active verbs govern the objective case: as, "I kissed *her*." "She scratched *me*." "Virtue rewards *her followers*."

For which reason she is like a cook.

Verbs neuter do not govern an objective case. Observe, therefore, that such phrases: as, "She *cried a good one*," "He *came the old soldier* over me," and so forth, are highly improper in a grammatical point of view, to say nothing of other objections to them.

These verbs, however, are capable of governing words of a meaning similar to their own: as, in the affecting ballad of Giles Scroggins—

"I wont, she cried, and *screamed a scream*."

The verb To Be has the same case after it as that which goes before it: as, "It was *I*," not "It was *me*." "The *Grubbs* were *they* who eat so much trifle at our last party;" not "The *Grubbses* were *them*."

RULE XII.

One verb governs another that depends upon it, in the infinitive mood: as, "Cease *to smoke* pipes." "Begin *to wear* collars." "I advise you *to shave*." "I recommend you *to go* to church." "I resolved *to visit* the United States.

> "And there I learned *to wheel* about
> And jump Jim Crow."

In general, the preposition *to* is used before the latter of two verbs; but sometimes it is more properly omitted: as, "I saw you *take* it, young fellow; come along with me." "Let me *get* hold of you, that's all!" "Did I hear you *speak*?" "I'll let you *know*!" "You dare not *hit* me." "Bid me *discourse*." "You need not *sing*."

The preposition *for* is sometimes unnecessarily intruded into a sentence, in addition to the preposition *to*, before an infinitive mood: as, "How came you *for* to think, *for* to go, *for* to do such a thing?" "Do you want me *for* to punch your head?"

Adjectives, substantives, and participles, often govern the infinitive mood: as, "Miss Hopkins, I shall be happy to dance the next set with you." "Oh! Sir, it is impossible to refuse you." "Have you an inclination to waltz?" "I shall be delighted in endeavouring to do so."

"NOT TO MINCE MATTERS, MISS, I LOVE YOU"

The infinitive mood is frequently made absolute, that is, independent of the rest of the sentence: as, "To say the truth, I was rather the worse for liquor." "Not to mince matters, Miss, I love you." "To begin at the right end." "To cut a long tale short," &c.

RULE XIII.

The relation which words and phrases bear to each other in point of time, should always be duly marked: instead of saying, "Last night I intended to have made strong love to her," we should say, "Last night I intended to make strong love to her;" because, although the intention of making strong love may have been abandoned (on reflection) this morning, and is now, therefore, a thing which is *past*, yet it is undoubtedly, when last night and the thoughts connected with it are brought back, again present to the mind.

RULE XIV.

Participles have the same power of government with that of the verbs from which they are derived: as, "Oh, what an exquisite singer Rubini is! I am so fond of *hearing him*." "Look at that horrid man; I declare he is *quizzing us*!" "No, he is only *taking snuff*." "See, how that thing opposite keeps *making eyes*." "Yes, she is *ogling Lumley*; I should so like to pinch her!" "How fond they all are of *wearing mustaches*! Don't you like it?" "Oh, yes! there is no *resisting them*." "Heigho! I am *dying to have* an ice—"

 ——Young man for a husband, Miss?
 For shame, Sir! don't be rude!

Participles are sometimes used as substantives: as, "The French mouth is adapted to *the making of* grimaces." "The cobbler is like the parson; he lives by *the mending of* soles." "The tailor reaps a good harvest from *the sewing of* cloth." "Did you ever see *a shooting of* the moon?"

Is this what the witches mean when they sing, in the acting play of Macbeth,

 "We *fly* by night?"

If *they* "shoot the moon," they are shooting *stars*.

There is a mode of using the indefinite article *a* before a participle, for which there is no occasion, as it does not convert the participle into a substantive, and makes no alteration in the sense of what is said; in this case the *article*, therefore, is like a wart, a wen, or a knob at the end of the nose, neither useful nor ornamental: as, "Going out *a* shooting." "Are you a coming to-morrow?" "I was *a* thinking about what Jem said." "Here you are, *a* going of it, as usual!"

A liberty not unfrequently taken with the English Language, is the substitution of the perfect participle for the imperfect tense, and of the imperfect tense for the perfect participle: as, "He *run* like mad, with the great dog after him." "Maria *come* and told us all about it." "When I had *wrote* the Valentine, I sealed it with my thimble." "He has *rose* to (be) a common-councilman." "I was *chose* Lord Mayor." "I've *eat* (or *a eat*) lots of venison in my time." "I should have *spoke* if you hadn't put in your oar." "You were *mistook*." "He sent her an affecting copy of verses, which was *wrote* with a Perryian pen."

RULE XV.

Adverbs are generally placed in a sentence before adjectives, after verbs active or neuter, and frequently between the auxiliary and the verb: as, "He came, Sir, and he *was most exceedingly drunk*; he *could hardly stand* upon his legs; he made a *very lame* discourse; he *spoke incoherently* and *ridiculously*; and *was impatiently heard* by the whole assembly." "He *is fashionably* dressed." "She *is conspicuously ugly*." "The eye of jealousy *is proverbially sharp*, and yet it *is indisputably green*." "Britons *may often be sold*, but they *will never be* slaves." "The French Marquis was a *very charming* man; he *danced exquisitely* and *nimbly*, and was *greatly admired* by all the ladies."

THE FRENCH MARQUIS

Several adverbs have been coined in America of late; and some of them are very remarkable for a "particular" elegance: as, "I reckon you're *catawampously chawed up.*"

In the example just given there is to be found, besides the new adverb, a word which, if not also new to the English student, is rendered so both by its orthography and pronunciation; namely, *chawed*. This term is no other than "chewed," modified (as words, like living things, would seem to be), by transportation to a foreign country. "Chawed up" is a very strong expression, and is employed to signify the most complete state of discomfiture and defeat, when a man is as much crushed, mashed, and comminuted, morally speaking, as if he had literally and corporeally undergone the process of mastication. "Catawampously" is a concentration of "hopelessly," "tremendously," "thoroughly," and "irrevocably;" so that "catawampously chawed up," means, brought as nearly to a state of utter annihilation as anything consistently with the laws of nature can possibly be. For the metaphorical use of the word "chawed," made by the Americans, three several reasons have been given: 1. Familiarity with the manner in which the alligator disposes of his victims. 2. The cannibalism of the Aborigines. 3. The delicate practice of chewing tobacco. Each of these is supported by numerous arguments, on the consideration of which it would be quite out of the question to enter in this place.

RULE XVI.

Two English negatives (like French lovers) destroy one another,—and become equivalent to an affirmative: as, "The question before the House was *not* an *unimportant* one;" that is, "it was an important one." "His Lordship was free to confess that he did *not* undertake to say that he would *not* on some future occasion give a satisfactory answer to the right honourable gentleman."

Thus, at one and the same time, we teach our readers Syntax and secretiveness.

It is probable that small boys are often unacquainted with this rule; for many of them, while undergoing personal chastisement, exclaim, for the purpose, as it would appear, of causing its duration to be shortened—"Oh pray, Sir, oh pray, Sir, oh pray, Sir! I *won't* do so *no* more!"

RULE XVII.

Prepositions govern the objective case: as, "What did the butcher say *of her*?" "He said that she would never do *for him*; that she was too thin *for a wife*, and he was not fond *of a spare rib*."

The delicate ear is much offended by any deviation from this rule: as, in a shocking and vulgar song which it was once our misfortune to hear:—

> "There I found the faithless she
> Frying sausages *for he.*"

As also in the conversation of rustics: as, "It's all one *to we*." "Come out *of they 'taters!*" "He went to the Parson's *with I*." "*From he to they* an't more nor dree mile."

We had occasion, in the Etymology, to remark on a certain misuse of the preposition, *of*. This, perhaps, is best explained by stating that *of*, in the instances cited, is made to usurp the government of cases which are already under a rightful jurisdiction: as, "*What* are you got a eating *of*?" "He had been a beating *of his wife*."

RULE XVIII.

Conjunctions connect similar moods and tenses of verbs, and cases of nouns and pronouns: as, "A coat of arms suspended on a wall is like an executed traitor; it *is hanged, drawn, and quartered*." "If you continue thus *to drink* brandy and water *and to smoke* cigars, you will be like Boreas the North wind, who *takes* 'cold without' wherever he goes, *and* always '*blows* a cloud' when it comes in his way." "Do you think there is any thing between *him and her*?" "Yes; *he and she* are engaged ones."

"THE ENGAGED ONES"

Note.—To ask whether there is any thing between two persons of opposite sexes, is one way of inquiring whether they are in love with each other. It is not, however, in our opinion, a very happy phrase, inasmuch as whatever intervenes between a couple of fond hearts, must tend to prevent them from coming together. Pyramus and Thisbe, as Ovid informs us, had more between them than they liked—a conjunction disjunctive in the shape of a wall. And by the bye, now that we are speaking of Pyramus and Thisbe, we may as well expend a word or two on a matter which, though of much interest, has never yet been noticed by the learned. Pyramus and Thisbe, it is well known, used to kiss each other through a hole in the wall which separated them. Now we have always been puzzled to imagine how they managed it. We are told by the Poet that they lived—

> "Ubi dicitur altam
> Coctilibus muris cinxisse Semiramis urbem"—

that is to say, where Semiramis is said to have surrounded a lofty city—not with *cock-tail mice*, as Mr. Canning facetiously translated "Coctilibus muris,"—but with *brick walls*. The wall which separated two adjoining houses must have been at least a brick thick; and although it be possible, "with Love's light wings" to "o'erperch" an exceedingly high wall, it occurs to us that it would be no easy thing for Love's long lips, let them be as long as you will, to reach through a moderately thick one. We do not know exactly what was the breadth of an Assyrian brick, but supposing it to have been three inches, an inch and a half of lip would have been required on the part of either lover for a kiss which could barely be sworn by;—a sort of presentation salute;—but for one worth giving or taking, we must allow an additional half inch of mouth to the gentleman. After all, their noses must have been so much in the way, that to make the operation at all feasible, either these features must have been particularly flat, or the aperture a very large one; whereas it is well known to have been merely a chink. Common observation on the part of their respective parents would have detected such a gap, and common prudence would have stopped it up. How, then, are we to reconcile Ovid's story with truth? Now, remember, reader, what has been said about noses and lips. Our deliberate opinion is that Pyramus and Thisbe were *a couple of negroes*. We shall be told that it is one utterly irreconcileable with the description of them given in the Metamorphoses. No matter—

> "The lunatic, the lover, and the poet,
> Are of imagination all compact."

And considering that the lover—

> "Sees Helen's beauty in a brow of Egypt,"

we do not see why Abyssinian charms should not be transformed by a poet into those of Assyria. And so, having proved (to our own satisfaction at least) that the beautiful Thisbe was a Hottentot Venus, we will resume the consideration of conjunctions.

RULE XIX.

Some conjunctions govern the indicative; some the subjunctive mood. In general, it is right to use the subjunctive, when contingency or doubt is implied: as, "*If I were* to say that the moon is made of green cheese." "*If I were* a wiseacre." "*If I were* a Wiltshire-man." "A lady, *unless she be toasted*, is never drunk."

And when she is toasted, those who are drunk are generally the gentlemen.

"THE LADIES!"

Those conjunctions which have a positive and absolute signification, require the indicative mood: as, "He who fasts may be compared to a horse: for *as* the animal *eats* not a bit, *so neither does* the man partake of a morsel." "The rustic is deluded by false hopes, *for* his daily food *is* gammon."

Every philosopher has his weak points, and in the Sylva Sylvarum may be found some *gammon of Bacon.*

RULE XX.

When a comparison is made between two or more things, the latter noun or pronoun is not governed by the conjunction *than* or *as*, but agrees with the verb, or is governed by the verb or preposition, expressed or understood: as, "The French are a lighter people than we," (that is "than we are,") "and yet we are not so dark as they," that is, "as they are." "I should think that they admire me more than them," that is, "than they admire them." "It is a shame, Martha! you were thinking more of that young officer than me," that is, "of me."

Sufficient attention is not always paid, in discourse, to this rule. Thus, a schoolboy may be often heard to exclaim, "What did you hit me for, you great fool?

you're bigger *than me.* Hit some one of your own size!" "Not fling farther *than him?* just can't I, that's all!" "You and I have got more marbles *than them.*"

"HIT ONE OF YOUR OWN SIZE!"

RULE XXI.

An ellipsis, or omission of certain words, is frequently allowed, for the sake of avoiding disagreeable repetitions, and of expressing our ideas in few words. Instead of saying "She was a little woman, she was a round woman, and she was an old woman," we say, making use of the figure Ellipsis, "She was a little, round, and old woman."

When, however, the omission of words is productive of obscurity, weakens the sentence, or involves a violation of some grammatical principle, the ellipsis must not be used. It is improper to say "Puddings fill who fill them;" we should supply the word *those.* "A beautiful leg of mutton and turnips" is not good language: those who would deserve what they are talking about ought to say, "A beautiful leg of mutton and fine turnips."

In common discourse, in which the meaning can be eked out by gestures, signs, and inarticulate sounds variously modified, the ellipsis is much more liberally and more extensively employed than in written composition. "May I have the pleasure of—hum? ha?" may constitute an invitation to take wine. "I shall be quite—a—a—" may serve as an answer in the affirmative. "So then, you see he was—eh!—you see——," is perhaps an intimation that a man has been hanged. "Well, of all the—I never!" is often tantamount to three times as many words expressive of surprise, approbation, or disapprobation, according to the tone in which it is uttered. "Will you?—ah!—will you?—ah!—ah!—ah!" will do either for "Will you be so impertinent, you scoundrel? will you dare to do so another time?" or, "Will you, dearest, loveliest, most adorable of your sex, will you consent to make me happy; will you be mine? speak! answer, I entreat you! One word from those sweet lips will make me the most fortunate man in existence!"

There is, however, a kind of ellipsis which those who indulge in that style of epistolary writing, wherein sentiments of a tender nature are conveyed, will do well to avoid with the greatest care. The ellipsis alluded to, is that of the first person singular of the personal pronoun, as instanced in the following model of a billet-doux:—

Camberwell,
April 1, 1840.

MY DEAREST FANNY,

Have not enjoyed the balm of sleep all the livelong night. Encountered, last night, at the ball, the beau ideal of my heart. Never knew what love was till then. Derided the sentiment often; jested at scars, because had never felt a wound. Feel at last the power of beauty—Write with a tremulous hand; waver between hope and fear. Hope to be thought not altogether unworthy of regard: fear to be rejected as having no pretensions to the affections of such unparalleled loveliness. Know not in what terms to declare my feelings. Adore you, worship you, dote on you, am wrapt up in you! think but on you, live but for you, would willingly die for you!—in short, love you! and imploring you to have some compassion on one who is distracted for your sake

Remain
Devotedly yours
T. TOUT.

RULE XXII.

A regular and dependent construction should be carefully preserved throughout the whole of a sentence, and all its parts should correspond to each other. There is, therefore, an inaccuracy in the following sentence; "Greenacre was more admired, but not so much lamented, as Burke." It should be, "Greenacre was more admired than Burke, but not so much lamented."

Of these two worthies there will be a notice of the following kind in a biographical dictionary, to be published a thousand years hence in America.

Greenacre.—A celebrated critic who so cut up a blue-stocking lady of the name of Brown, that he did not leave her a leg to stand upon.

Burke.—A famous orator, whose power of stopping people's mouths was said to be prodigious. It is farther reported of him that he was only once hung up, and that on the occasion of the last speech he ever made.

Perhaps it may be said that the rule last stated comprehends all preceding rules, and requires exemplification accordingly. We therefore call the attention of the reader to the following paragraph, requesting him to consider what, and how many, violations of the maxims of Syntax it contains.

> "We teaches, that is, my son and me teaches, they boys English Grammar. Tom or Dick have learned something every day but Harry what is idler, whom I am sure will never come to no good, for he is always a miching and doing those kind of things (he was catch but yesterday in a skittle grounds) he only makes his book all dog's ears. I beat he, too, pretty smartish, as I ought, you will say, for to have did. I was going to have sent him away last week but he somehow got over me as he do always. I have had so much trouble with he, that between you and I, if I was not paid for it, I wouldn't have no more to do with such a boy. There never wasn't a monkey more mischievious than him; and a donkey isn't more stupider and not half so obstinate as that youngster."

The Syntax of the Interjection has been sufficiently stated under Rule V. Interjections afford more matter for consideration in a Treatise on Elocution than they do in a work on Grammar; but there is one observation which we are desirous of making respecting them, and which will not, it is hoped, be thought altogether foreign to our present subject. Almost every interjection has a great variety of meanings, adapted to particular occasions and circumstances, and indicated chiefly by the tone of the voice. Of this proposition we shall now give a few illustrations, which we would endeavour to render still clearer by the addition of musical notes, but that these would hardly express, with adequate exactness, the modulations of sound to which we allude; and besides, we hope to be sufficiently understood without such help. This part of the Grammar should be read aloud by the student; or, which is better still, the interjection, where it is possible, should be repeated with the proper intonation by a class; the sentence which gives occasion to it being read by the preceptor. We will select the interjection Oh! as the source from which our examples are to be drawn.

"I'll give it you, you idle dog: I will!"

"Oh, pray, Sir! Oh, pray, Sir! Oh! Oh! Oh!"

"I shall ever have the highest esteem for you, Sir; but as to love, that is out of the question."

"Oh, Matilda!"

"I say, Jim, look at that chaffinch: there's a shy!"

"Oh, Crikey!"

"Miss Tims, do you admire Lord Byron?"

"Oh, yes!"

"What do you think of Rubini's singing?"

"Oh!"

"So then, you see, we popped round the corner, and caught them just in the nick of time."

"Oh!"

"Sir, your behaviour has done you great credit."

"Oh!"

"Oats are looking up."

"Oh!"

"Honourable Members might say what they pleased; but he was convinced, for his part, that the New Poor Law had given great general satisfaction."

"Oh! oh!"

There being now no reason (or rule) to detain us in the Syntax, we shall forthwith advance into Prosody, where we shall have something to say, not only about rules, but also of measures.

PART IV.
PROSODY.

PART IV.

PROSODY.

Prosody consists of two parts; wherefore, although it may be a topic, a head, or subject for discussion, it can never be a point; for a *point* is that which hath *no* parts. Besides, there are a great many *lines* to be considered in the second part of Prosody, which treats of Versification. The first division teaches the true Pronunciation of Words, including Accent, Quantity, Emphasis, Pause, and Tone.

Lord Chesterfield's book about manners, which is intended to teach us the proper *tone* to be adopted in Society, may be termed an Ethical Prosody.

Lord Chesterfield may have been a polished gentleman, but Dr. Johnson was of the two the more shining character.

CHAPTER I.

OF PRONUNCIATION.

SECTION I.
OF ACCENT.

Though *penetrated* ourselves by the desire of imparting instruction, we are far from wishing to *bore* our readers; and therefore we shall endeavour to repeat nothing here that we have said before.

Accent is the marking with a peculiar stress of the voice a particular letter or syllable in a word, in such a manner as to render it more distinct or audible than the rest. Thus, in the word *théatre*, the stress of the voice should be on the letter *e* and first syllable *the*; and in *cóntrary*, on the first syllable *con*. How shocking it is to hear people say *con-tráry, the-átre*! The friends of education will be reminded with regret, that an error in the pronunciation of the first of these words is very early impressed on the human mind.

> "Mary, Mary,
> Quite contráry,
> How does your garden grow?"

How many evils, alas! arise from juvenile associations!

Words of two syllables never have more than one of them accented, except for the sake of peculiar emphasis. Gentlemen, however, whose profession it is to drive certain public vehicles called cabs, are much accustomed to disregard this rule, and to say, "pó-líte" (or "púr-líte"), "gén-téel," "cón-cérn," "pó-líce," and so on: nay, they go so far as to convert a word of one syllable into two, for the sake of indulging in this style of pronunciation; and thus the word "queer" is pronounced by them as "ké-véer."

The word "á-mén," when standing alone, should be pronounced with two accents.

The accents in which it usually *is* pronounced are very inelegant. Clerks, now-a-days, alas! are no scholars.

Dissyllables, formed by adding a termination, usually have the former syllable accented: as, "Fóolish, blóckhead," &c.

The accent in dissyllables, formed by prefixing a syllable to the radical word, is commonly on the latter syllable: as, "I protést, I decláre, I entréat, I adóre, I expíre."

ALL FOR LOVE

Protestations, declarations, entreaties, and adorations, proclaim a swain to be simply tender; but *expiration* (for love) proves him to be decidedly soft.

A man who turns lover becomes a *protest*-ant; and his conduct at the same time generally undergoes a *reformation*, especially if he has previously been a rake.

The zeal, however, of a reformed rake, like that of Jack in Dean Swift's "Tale of a Tub," is sometimes apt to outrun his discretion.

When the same word, being a dissyllable, is both a noun and a verb, the verb has mostly the accent on the latter, and the noun on the former syllable: as,

> "Molly, let Hymen's gentle hand
> Cemént our hearts together,
> With such a cément as shall stand
> In spite of wind and weather.

"I do preságe—and oft a fact
A présage doth foretoken—
Our mutual love shall ne'er contráct,
Our cóntract ne'er be broken."

"TALE OF A TUB"

There are many exceptions to the rule just enunciated (so that, correctly as well as familiarly speaking, it is perhaps *no* rule); for though verbs seldom have an accent on the former, yet nouns frequently have it on the latter syllable: as,

"Mary Anne is my delíght
Both by day and eke by night;
For by day her soft contról
Soothes my heart and calms my soul;
And her image while I doze

> Comes to sweeten my repóse;
> Fortune favouring my desígn,
> Please the pigs she shall be mine!"

The former syllable of most dissyllables ending in *y, our, ow, le, ish, ck, ter, aye, en, et,* is accented: as, "Gránny, nóodle," &c.

Except allów, avów, endów, bestów, belów.

> "Sir, I cannot allów
> You your flame to avów;
> Endów yourself first with the rhino:
> My hand to bestów
> On a fellow belów
> Me!—I'd rather be—never mind—
> *I* know."

"Music," in the language of the Gods, is sometimes pronounced "mú-síc!"

Nouns of two syllables ending in *er,* have the accent on the former syllable: as, "Bútcher, báker."

It is, perhaps, a singular thing, that persons who pursue the callings denoted by the two words selected as examples, should always indicate their presence at an area by crying out, in direct defiance of Prosody, "But-chér, ba-kér;" the latter syllable being of the two the more strongly accented.

Dissyllabic verbs ending in a consonant and e final, as "Disclose," "repine," or having a diphthong in the last syllable, as, "Believe," "deceive," or ending in two consonants, as "Intend," are accented on the latter syllable.

> "Matilda's eyes a light disclóse,
> Which with the star of Eve might vie;
> Oh! that such lovely orbs as those
> Should sparkle at an apple-pie!

> "Thy love I thought was wholly mine,
> Thy heart I fondly hoped to rule;
> Its throne I cannot but repíne
> At sharing with a goosb'ry fool!

> "Thou swear'st no flatterer can decéive
> Thy mind,—thy breast no coxcomb rifle;
> Thou art no trifler, I beliéve,
> But why so plaguy fond of trifle?

> "Why, when we're wed—I don't inténd
> To joke, Matilda, or be funny;
> I really fear that you will spend
> The Honey Moon in eating honey!"

Most dissyllabic nouns, having a diphthong in the latter syllable, have the accent also on that syllable: as,

> "A Hamlet that draws
> Is sure of appláuse."

A Hamlet that *draws*? There are not many who can give even an outline of the character.

In a few words ending in *ain* the accent is placed on the former syllable: as, "Víllain," which is pronounced as the natives of Whitechapel pronounce "willing."

Those dissyllables, the vowels of which are separated in pronunciation, always have the accent on the first syllable: as, lion, scion, &c.

> When is a young and tender shoot
> Like a fond swain? When 'tis a *scíon*.
> What's the most gentlemanly brute
> Like, of all flow'rs? A *dandy* líon.

Trisyllables, formed by adding a termination or prefixing a syllable, retain the accent of the radical word: as, "Lóveliness, shéepishness, Whíggery, knávery, assúrance."

The first syllable of trisyllables ending in *ous, al, ion,* is accented in the generality of cases: as in the words "sérious, cápital," &c.

> "Dr. Johnson declared, with a sérious face,
> That he reckoned a punster a villain:
> What would he have thought of the horrible case
> Of a man who makes jokes that are *killing*?

> "In his díction to speak 'tis not easy for one
> Who must furnish both reason and rhyme;
> Sir, the rogue who has utter'd a cápital pun,
> Has committed a cápital crime."

Trisyllables ending in *ce, ent, ate, y, re, le,* and *ude,* commonly accent the first syllable. Many of those, however, which are derived from words having the accent on the last syllable, and of those of which the middle syllable has a vowel between two consonants, are excepted.

> They who would elegantly speak
> Should not say "ímpudence," but "cheek;"
> Should all things éatable call "prog;"
> Eyes "ogles," cóuntenance "phisog."
> A coach should nóminate a "drag,"
> And spécify as "moke," a nag:
> For éxcellent, use "prime" or "bang up,"
> Or "out and out;" and "scrag," for hang up.
> The théatre was wont to teach
> The public réctitude of speech,
> But we who live in modern age
> Consult the gallery, not the stage.

Trisyllables ending in *ator* have the accent placed on the middle syllable; as, "Spectátor, narrátor," &c. except órator, sénator, and a few other words.

Take care that you never pronounce the common name of the vegetable sometimes called Irish wall-fruit, "purtátor."

A diphthong in the middle syllable of a trisyllable is accented: as also, in general, is a vowel before two consonants: as, "Doméstic," "endéavour."

An endeavour to appear domesticated, or in common phraseology, to "do" the domestic, is sometimes made by young gentlemen, and generally with but an ill grace. Avoid such attempts, reader, on all occasions: and in particular never adventure either to nurse babies, or (when you shall have "gone up to the ladies") to pour water into the tea-pot from the kettle. A legal or medical student sometimes thinks proper, from a desire of appearing at once gallant and facetious, to usurp the office of pouring out the tea itself, on which occasions he is very apt to betray his uncivilised habits by an unconscious but very unequivocal manipulation used in giving malt liquor what is technically termed a "head."

"A RESPECTABLE MAN."

Many polysyllables are regulated as to accent by the words from which they are derived: as, "Inexpréssibles, Súbstituted, Unobjéctionably, Désignated, Transatlántic, Délicacy, Decídedly, Unquéstionable."

Words ending in *ator* are commonly accented on the last syllable but one, let them be as long as they may: as, respirátor, regulátor, renovátor, indicátor, and all the other *ators* that we see in the newspapers.

A cockney, quoting Dr. Johnson, said, "Sir, I love a good *ator*."

Words that end in *le* usually have the accent on the first syllable: as, "Ámicable, déspicable," &c.: although we *have* heard people say "despícable." "I never see such a despícable fellow, not in all my born days."

Words of this class, however, the second syllable of which has a vowel before two consonants, are often differently accented: as in "Respéctable, contémptible."

Many words ending in *ion, ous, ty, ia, io,* and *cal,* have their accent on the last syllable but two: as, "Con-si-de-rá-ti-on, pro-dí-gi-ous, im-pe-ne-tra-bíl-i-ty, en-cy-clo-pæ´-di-a, brag-ga-dó-ci-o, an-ti-mo-nárch-i-cal," all of which words we have divided into syllables, by way of a hint that they are to be pronounced (comically speaking) after the manner of Dominie Sampson.

Having, in compliance with grammatical usage, laid down certain rules with regard to accent, we have to inform the reader that there are so many exceptions to almost all of them, that perhaps there is scarcely one which it is worth while to attend to. We hope we have in some measure amused him; but as to instruction, we fear that, in this part of our subject, we have given him very little of that. Those who would acquire a correct accent had better attend particularly to the mode of speaking adopted in good society; avoid debating clubs; and go to church. For farther satisfaction and information we refer them, and we beg to say that we are not joking—to *Walker*.

<h2 style="text-align:center">SECTION II.
OF QUANTITY.</h2>

The quantity of a syllable means the time taken up in pronouncing it. As there is in Arithmetic a long division and a short division, so in Prosody is Quantity considered as long or short.

A syllable is said to be long, when the accent is on the vowel, causing it to be slowly joined in pronunciation to the next letter: as, "Flēa, smāll, crēature."

A syllable is called short, when the accent lies on the consonant, so that the vowel is quickly joined to the succeeding letter: as "Crăck, lĭttle, dĕvil."

The pronunciation of a long syllable commonly occupies double the time of a short one: thus, "Pāte," and "Brōke," must be pronounced as slowly again as "Păt," and "Knŏck."

We have remarked a curious tendency in the more youthful students of Grammar to regard the quantity of words (in their lessons) more as being "small" or "great" than as coming under the head of "long" or "short." Their predilection for small quantities of words is very striking and peculiar; food for the mind they seem to look upon as physic; and all physic, in their estimation, is most agreeably taken in infinitesimal doses. The Homœopathic system of acquiring knowledge is more to their taste than even the Hamiltonian.

It is quite impossible to give any rules as to quantity worth reading. The Romans may have submitted to them, but that is no reason why we should. We will pronounce our words as we please: and if foreigners want to know why, we will tell them that, when there is no Act of Parliament to the contrary, an Englishman always does as he likes with his own.

DOING WHAT YOU LIKE WITH YOUR OWN

SECTION III.
OF EMPHASIS.

Emphasis is the distinguishing of some word or words in a sentence, on which we wish to lay particular stress, by a stronger and fuller sound, and sometimes by a particular tone of the voice.

A few illustrations of the importance of emphasis will be, perhaps, both agreeable and useful.

When a young lady says to a young gentleman, "You are a *nice* fellow; you *are!*" —she means one thing.

When a young gentleman, addressing one of his own sex, remarks, "*You*'re a nice fellow; *you* are;" —he means another thing.

"Your friend is a gentleman," pronounced without any particular emphasis, is the simple assertion of a fact.

"Your *friend* is a *gentleman*," with the emphasis on the words "friend" and "gentleman," conveys an insinuation besides.

So simple a question as "Do you like pine-apple rum?" is susceptible of as many meanings as there are words in it; according to the position of the emphasis.

"*Do* you like pine-apple rum?" is as much as to say, "Do you, though, really like pine-apple rum?"

"Do *you* like pine-apple rum?" is tantamount to, "Can it be that a young gentleman (or lady) like you, can like pine-apple rum?"

"Do you *like* pine-apple rum?" means, "Is it possible that instead of disliking, you are fond of pine-apple rum?"

"Do you like *pine-apple* rum?" is an enquiry as to whether you like that kind of rum in particular.

And lastly, "Do you like pine-apple *rum*?" is equivalent to asking if you think that the flavour of the pine-apple improves that especial form of alcohol.

A well-known instance of an emphasis improperly placed was furnished by a certain Parson, who read a passage in the Old Testament in the following unlucky manner: "And he said unto his sons, Saddle me the ass; and they saddled *him*."

Young ladies are usually very emphatic in ordinary discourse. "What a little *dear*! *Oh!* how *sweetly* pretty! Well! I never *did*, I declare! *So* nice, and *so* innocent, and *so* good-tempered, and *so* affectionate, and *such* a colour! And *oh! such lovely eyes!* and such hair! He *was* a little duck! he *was*, he *was*, he *was*. Tzig a tzig, tzig, tzig, tzig, tzig!" &c. &c. &c.

This emphatic way of speaking is indicative of two very amiable feelings implanted by nature in the female occiput, and called by the Phrenologists Adhesiveness and Philoprogenitiveness. Those who attempt to imitate it will be conscious, while forcing out their words, of a peculiar mental emotion, which we cannot explain otherwise than by saying, that it is analogous to that which attends the act of pressing or squeezing; as when, with the thumb of the right hand, we knead one lump of putty to another, in the palm of the left. Perhaps we might also instance, sucking an orange. In all these cases, the organ of Weight, according to Phrenology, is also active; and this, perhaps, is one of the faculties which induce young ladies to lay a stress upon their words. Nevertheless, we fear that a damsel would hardly be pleased by being told that her *weight* was considerable, though it would, at the same time, grievously offend her to accuse her of *lightness*. Here we need scarcely observe, that we refer to lightness, not of complexion, but of sentiment, which is always regarded as a *dark* shade in the character. This defect, we think, we may safely assert, will never be observed in emphatic fair ones.

"WHAT A LITTLE DEAR!"

But we have not yet quite exhausted the subject of emphasis, considered in relation to young ladies. Their letters are as emphatic as their language is, almost every third word being underlined. Such epistles, inasmuch as they are addressed to the heart, ought not to be submitted to the ear; nevertheless we must say that we have occasionally been wicked and waggish enough to read them aloud—to ourselves alone, of course. The reader may, if he choose, follow our example. We subjoin a specimen of female correspondence, endeared to us by many tender recollections, and admirably adapted to our present purpose.

My *dear Paul,*

When we left *Town* on *Wednesday last* the weather was so very *rainy* that we were *obliged* to have the *coach windows* up. I was *terribly* afraid that *Matilda* and I would have caught our *Death* of *cold*; but thank *Goodness* no such *untoward* event took place. It was *very uncomfortable*, and I *so* wished *you had been there.* When we got *home* who *do you think* was there? Mr. *Sims*; and he *said* he *thought* that I was *so* much *grown.* Only *think.* And so then you know we took some *refreshment*, for *I assure* you, what with the *journey* and *altogether* we were very *nearly famished*; and we were *all invited* to go to the *Chubbs'* that *Evening* to a small *Tea Party*, for which I *must own* I *thought Mr. Chubb a nice man.* After tea we had a *carpet waltz*, and although I was *very tired* I *enjoyed* it *much.* There were some *very pretty girls* there, and *one* or *two agreeable young men*; but *oh!* &c.

The remainder of this letter being of a nature personally interesting to ourselves only, and likely, in the opinion of some readers, to render its insertion attributable to motives of vanity, we shall not be found fault with for objecting to transcribe any more of it.

SECTION IV.
OF PAUSES.

A Pause, otherwise called a rest, is an absolute cessation of the voice, in speaking or reading, during a perceptible interval, longer or shorter, of time.

Comic Pauses often occur in Oratory. "Unaccustomed as I am to public speaking," is usually followed by a pause of this sort. A young gentleman, his health having been drunk at a party, afforded, in endeavouring to return thanks, a signal illustration of the Pause Comic. "Gentlemen," he began, "the Ancient Romans," — (A pause), — "I say, Gentlemen, the Ancient Romans," — (Hear!) — "The Ancient Romans, Gentlemen," — (Bravo! hear! hear!) — "Gentlemen — that is — the Ancient Romans" — "were very fine fellows, Jack, I dare say," added a friend, pulling the speaker down by the coat-tail.

That notable Ancient Roman, Brutus, is represented by Shakspere as making a glorious pause: as,

"Who's here so vile that would not love his country? If any, speak, for him have I offended. I pause for a reply."

Here, of course, Brutus pauses, folds his arms, and looks magnanimous. We have heard, though, of an idle and impudent schoolboy, who, at a public recitation, when he had uttered the words "I pause for a reply," gravely took out his penknife and began paring his nails.

This *was* minding his *paws* with a vengeance.

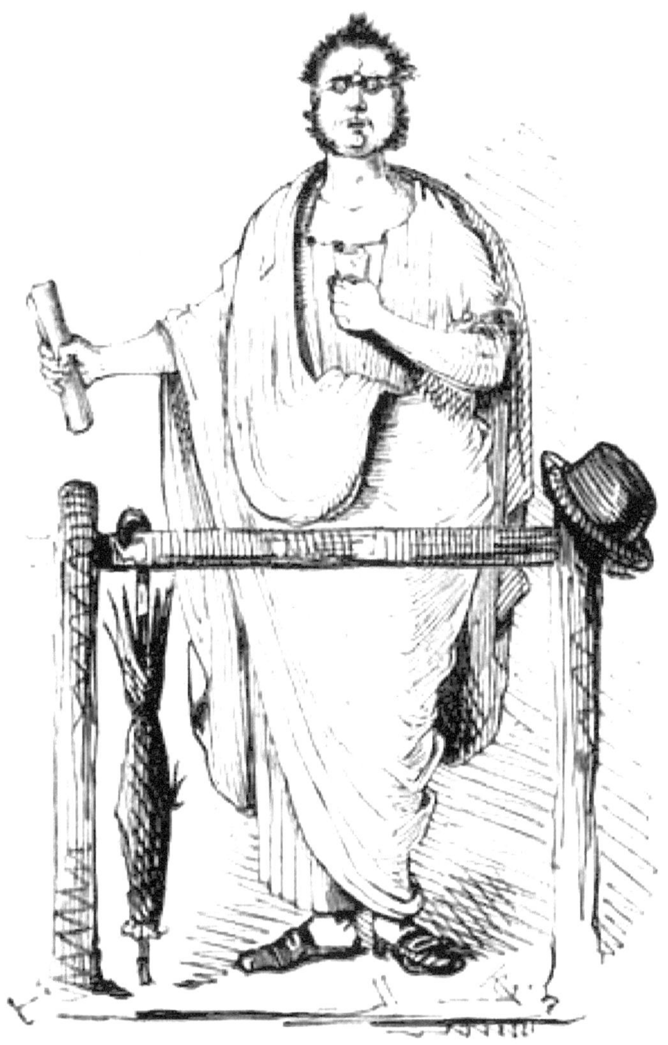

BRUTUS

A very long pause, particularly accompanied by a very serious look on the part of the speaker, as good as tells the audience that something of great importance is coming. It is therefore necessary to have something of real consequence to bring out. The following extract from a political harangue will show how essential it is to attend to this point:—

"And, Gentlemen, when I consider, I say, when I consider the condition of the masses of this country, I do think, and it is my opinion, that the Government has much to answer for. But not to dwell on that point, what have been the deeds, what have been the proceedings, I may say, of the Government itself? They have increased taxation, they have swelled the National Debt, they have assailed the liberty of the subject, they have trampled the poor man in the dust; he asked for liberty, and they made him a slave; he demanded the Charter, and they loaded him with fetters; he knelt for protection, and they gave him the Poor Law; he cried for bread, and they gave him the bayonet. By what name, by what term, by what expression, are we to designate such tyranny? (A long pause) ... Gentlemen!—it is *unconstitutional*!!!"

SECTION V.
OF TONES.

Tones consist of the modulations of the voice, or the notes or variations of sound which we use in speaking: thus differing materially both from emphasis and pauses.

An interesting diversity of *tones* is exhibited by the *popular voice* at an election.

Also by dust-men, milk-women, and pot-boys; and by fruiterers, hearth-stone-venders, ballad-singers, Last-Dying-Speech-hawkers, and old clothesmen itinerant.

We cannot exactly write tones (though it is easy enough to write notes), but we shall nevertheless endeavour to give some idea of their utility.

A lover and a police-magistrate (unless the two characters should chance to be combined, which sometimes happens, that is, when the latter is a lover of justice) would say, "Answer me," in very different tones.

Observe, that two doves billing resemble two magistrates bowing;—because they are beak to beak.

THE TWO DOVES

A lover again would utter the words "For ever and ever," in a very different tone from that in which a Parish Clerk would repeat them.

A young lady, on her first introduction to you, says, "Sir," in a tone very unlike that in which she sometime afterwards delivers herself of the same monosyllable when she is addressing you under the influence of jealousy.

As to the word "Sir," the number of constructions which, according to the tone in which it is spoken, it may be made to bear, are incalculable. We may adduce a few instances.

"Please, Sir, let me off my imposition."

"No, Sir!"

"Waiter! you, Sir."

"Yes, Sir! yes, Sir!"

"Sir, I am greatly obliged to you."

"Sir, you are quite welcome."

"Your servant, Sir" (by a man who brings you a challenge).

"'Servant, Sir" (by a tailor bowing you to the door).

"Sir, you are a gentleman!"

"Sir, you are a scoundrel!"

We need not go on with examples ad infinitum. If after what we have said anybody does not understand the nature of Tone, all we shall say of him is, that he is a *Tony* Lumpkin.

CHAPTER II.

OF VERSIFICATION.

Hurrah!

It is with peculiar pleasure that we approach this part of Prosody; and we have therefore prefaced it with an exclamation indicative of delight. We belong to a class of persons to whom a celebrated phrenological manipulator ascribes "some poetical feeling, if studied or called forth;" and, to borrow another expression from the same quarter, we sometimes "versify a little;" that is to say, we *diversify* our literary occupations by an occasional flirtation with the muses. Now it gives us great concern to observe that popular literature is becoming very prosaic. Poetry and Boxing have gone out of favour together, and most probably,—though we have not quite time enough just at present to show how,—from the same cause; namely, bad taste. We mention Boxing along with Poetry, because it is remarkable that their decline should have been contemporaneous; and because we are of those who believe that there exists an essential similarity between all the branches of the Fine Arts; and moreover, because—and we mention it as a fact no less singular in itself than creditable to the paper in question—that a celebrated weekly periodical bestows especial patronage on both. With regard to Boxing, we are glad to see that a few patriotic individuals have of late been endeavouring to revive the taste for it; and we have some hope that their exertions, backed by certain cases of stabbing which every now and then occur, will eventually prove successful. But no one can be found to labour in an equal degree for the advancement of poetry. Our innate modesty is prompting us to say, that we fear we can do but little in the cause; but early impressions are known to be very strong and lasting: and we have a notion that, in teaching youth to make verses, we shall in a great degree contribute to the breeding up of a race of poets, and thereby secure, not only laurels, at least, for them, but also gratitude, veneration, and all that kind of thing, for ourselves.

We have a great respect for the memory of our old schoolmaster; notwithstanding which, we think we can beat him (which, we shall be told by the wags, would be tit for tat) at poet-making, though, indeed, he was a magician in his way. "I'll make thee a poet, my boy," he used to say, "or the rod shall."

Let us try what *we* can do.

A verse consists of a certain number and variety of syllables, put together and arranged according to certain laws.

Verses being also called dulcet strains, harmonious numbers, tuneful lays, and so forth, it is clear that such combination and arrangement must be so made as to please the ear.

Versification is the making of verses. This seems such a truism as to be not worth stating; but it is necessary to define what Versification is, because many people suppose it to be the same thing with poetry. We will prove that it is not.

> "Much business in the Funds has lately been
> Transacted various monied men between;
> Though speculation early in the week
> Went slowly; nought was done whereof to speak.
> The largest operations, it was found,
> Were twenty-five and fifty thousand *pound*;
> The former in reduced Annuities,
> And in the Three per Cents. the last of these."

We might proceed in the same strain, but we have already done eight verses without a particle of poetry in them; and we do not wish to overwhelm people with proofs of what a great many will take upon trust.

Every fool knows what Rhyme is; so we need not say anything about that.

OF POETICAL FEET.

Poetical feet! Why, Fanny Elsler's feet and Taglioni's feet are poetical feet—are they not? or else what is meant by calling dancing the Poetry of Motion? And cannot each of those *artistes* boast of a toe which is the very essence of all poetry—a ΤΟ᾽ ΚΑΛΟ᾽Ν?

No. You may make verses *on* Taglioni's feet, (though if she be a poetess, she can do that better than you, standing, too, on one leg, like the man that Horace speaks of); but you cannot make them *of* her feet. Feet *of* which verses are composed are made of syllables, not of bones, muscles, and ligaments.

Feet and pauses are the constituent parts of a verse.

We have heard one boy ask another, who was singing, "How much is that a yard?" still the yard is not a poetical measure.

The feet which are used in poetry consist either of two or of three syllables. There are four kinds of feet of two, and an equal number of three syllables. Four and four are eight: therefore Pegasus is an octoped; and if our readers do not understand this logic, we are sorry for it. But as touching the feet—we have

1. The Trochee, which has the first syllable accented, and the last unaccented: as, "Yānkĕe dōodlĕ."

2. The Iambus, which has the first syllable unaccented, and the last accented: as, "Thĕ māid hĕrsēlf wĭth roūge, ălās! bĕdaūbs."

3. The Spondee, which has both the words or syllables accented: as, "Āll hāil, grēat kīng, Tōm Thūmb, āll hāil!"

4. The Pyrrhic, which has both the words or syllables unaccented: as, "Ŏn thĕ tree-top."

5. The Dactyl, which has the first syllable accented and the two latter unaccented: as, "Jŏnăthăn, Jĕffĕrsŏn."

6. The Amphibrach has the first and last syllables unaccented and the middle one accented: as, "Oĕ'rwĥelmĭng, trănspōrtĕd, ĕcstātĭc, dĕlīghtfŭl, ăccēptĕd, ăddrēssĕs."

7. The Anapæst (or as we used to say, *Nasty-beast*) has the two first syllables unaccented and the last accented: as, "Ŏvĕrgrōwn grĕnădiēr."

8. The Tribrach has all its syllables unaccented: as, "Matrĭmŏnў, exquĭsĭtenĕss."

These feet are divided into *principal* feet, out of which pieces of poetry may be wholly or chiefly formed; and *secondary* feet, the use of which is to diversify the number and improve the verse.

We shall now proceed to explain the nature of the principal feet.

Iambic verses are of several kinds, each kind consisting of a certain number of feet or syllables.

1. The shortest form of the English Iambic consists of an Iambus, with an additional short syllable, thus coinciding with the Amphibrach: as,

> "Whăt, Sūsăn,
> My beauty!
> Refuse one
> So true t' ye?
> This ditty
> Of sadness
> Begs pity
> For madness."

2. The second form of the English Iambic consists of *two* Iambuses, and sometimes takes an additional short syllable: as,

> "Mў eӯe, whăt fūn,
> With dog and gun,
> And song and shout,
> To roam about!
> And shoot our snipes!
> And smoke our pipes!
> Or eat at ease,
> Beneath the trees,
> Our bread and cheese!
> To rouse the hare
> From gloomy lair;
> To scale the mountain
> And ford the fountain,
> While rustics wonder
> To hear our thunder."

Everybody has heard of the "Cockney School," of course.

3. The third form consists of *three* Iambuses: as in the following *morceau*, the author of which is, we regret to say, unknown to us; though we *did* once hear somebody say that it was a Mr. Anon.

> "Jăck Sprāt ĕat āll thĕ fāt,
> His wife eat all the lean,
> And so between them both,
> They lick'd the platter clean."

In this verse an additional short syllable is also admitted: as,

> "Ălēxĭs, yoūthfŭl ploūgh-bŏy,
> A shepherdess adored,
> Who loved fat Hodge, the cow-boy,
> So t'other chap was floored."

4. The fourth form is made up of four Iambuses: as,

> "Ădieū mў bōots, cŏmpāniŏns ōld,
> New footed twice, and four times soled;
> My footsteps ye have guarded long,
> Life's brambles, thorns, and flints among;
> And now you're past the cobbler's art,
> And Fate declares that we must part.
> Ah me! what cordial can restore
> The gaping patch repatch'd before?
> What healing art renew the weal
> Of subject so infirm of heel?
> What potion, pill, or draught control
> So deep an ulcer of the *sole*?"

5. The fifth species of English Iambic consists of *five* Iambuses: as,

> "Cŏme, Trāgĭc Mūse, ĭn tāttĕr'd vēst ărrāy'd,
> And while through blood, and mud, and crimes I wade,
> Support my steps, and this, my strain, inspire
> With Horror's blackest thoughts and bluest fire!"

The Epic of which the above example is the opening, will perhaps appear hereafter. This kind of Iambic constitutes what is called the Heroic measure:—of which we shall have more to say by and by; but shall only remark at present that it, in common with most of the ordinary English measures, is susceptible of many varieties, by the admission of other feet, as Trochees, Dactyls, Anapæsts, &c.

6. Our Iambic in its sixth form, is commonly called the Alexandrine measure. It consists of six Iambuses: as,

> "Hĭs wōrshĭp gāve thĕ wōrd, ănd Snōoks wăs bōrne ăwāy."

The Alexandrine is sometimes introduced into heroic rhyme, and when used, as the late Mr. John Reeve was wont to say, "with a little moderation," occasions an agreeable variety. Thus, the example quoted is preceded by the following lines:—

> "What! found at midnight with a darkey, lit,

> A bull-dog, jemmy, screw, and centre-bit
> And tongueless of his aim? It cannot be
> But he was bent, at least, on felony;
> He stands remanded. 'Ho! Policeman A!'
> His Worship gave the word, and Snooks was borne away."

7. The seventh and last form of our Iambic measure is made up of *seven* Iambuses. This species of verse has been immortalised by the adoption of those eminent hands, Messrs. Sternhold and Hopkins. It runs thus:—

> "Good people all, I pray draw near, for you I needs must tell,
> That William Brown is dead and gone; the man you knew full well.
> A broad brimm'd hat, black breeches, and an old Welch wig he wore:
> And now and then a long brown coat all button'd up before."

The present measure is as admirably adapted for the Platform as for the Conventicle.

> "My name it is Bill Scroggins, and my fate it is to die,
> For I was at the Sessions tried and cast for felony.
> My friends, to these my dying words I pray attention lend,
> The public-house has brought me unto this untimely end."

Verses of this kind are now usually broken into two lines, with four feet in the first line, and three in the second: as,

> "I wish I were a little pig
> To wallow in the mire,
> To eat, and drink, and sleep at ease
> Is all that I desire."

Trochaic verse is of several kinds.

1. The shortest Trochaic verse in the English language consists of one Trochee and a long syllable: as,

> "Billy Black
> Got the sack."

Lindley Murray asserts that this measure is defective in dignity, and can seldom be used on serious occasions. Yet it is Pope who thus sings:

> "Dreadful screams,
> Dismal gleams.
> Fires that glow,
> Shrieks of woe," &c.

And for our own poor part, let us see what we can make out of a storm.

> "See the clouds
> Like to shrouds
> All so dun,
> Hide the Sun;
> Daylight dies;

Winds arise;
Songsters quake,
'Midst the brake;
Shepherds beat
Swift retreat:
"Lo you there!
High in air
Whirlwinds snatch
Tiles and thatch!
Steeple nods!
Oh! ye Gods!
Hark!—that bang!—
Brazen clang!
There the bell
Thund'ring fell!
Thunder rolls—
Save our souls!—
Welkin glares—
Lightning flares,
While it splits
Oak to bits—
Hail comes down—
Oh, my crown!
Patter crack!
Clatter whack!
How it pours!
Ocean roars,
Earth replies—
Mind your eyes—
Here's a cave—
Oh! that's brave!
Gracious Powers
Safety's ours!"

2. The second English form of the Trochaic consists of two feet: as,

"Vērmĭcēllĭ,
Cūrrănt jēllў."

It sometimes contains two feet, or trochees, with an additional long syllable: as,

"Yoūth ĭnclīned tŏ wēd,
Go and shave thy head."

3. The third species consists of three trochees: as,

"Sīng ă sŏng ŏf sīxpĕnce."

or of three trochees, with an additional long syllable: as,

"Thrīce mў cōat, hăve ō'er thĕe rōll'd,
Summer hot and winter cold,
Since the Snip's creative art
Into being bade thee start;

"Now like works the most sublime,
Thou display'st the power of Time.
Broad grey patches plainly trace,
Right and left each blade-bone's place;
When thy shining collar's scann'd,
Punsters think on classic land:
Thread-bare sleeves thine age proclaim,
Elbows worn announce the same;
Elbows mouldy-black of hue,
Save where white a crack shines through;
While thy parting seams declare
Thou'rt unfit for farther wear—
Then, farewell! "What! Moses! ho!"
"Clo', Sir? clo', Sir? clo', Sir? clo'?"

4. The fourth Trochaic species consists of four trochees: as,

"Ūgh! yŏu līttlĕ lūmp ŏf blūbbĕr,
Sleep, oh! sleep in quiet, do!
Cease awhile your bib to slobber—
Cease your bottle mouth to screw.

"How I wish your eyelids never
Would unclose again at all;
For I know as soon as ever
You're awake, you're sure to squall.

"Dad and Mammy's darling honey,
Tomb-stone cherub, stuff'd with slops,
Let each noodle, dolt, and spooney
Smack, who will, your pudding chops.

"As for me, as soon I'd smother,
As I'd drown a sucking cat,
You, you cub, or any other
Nasty little squalling brat."

This form may take an additional long syllable, but this measure is very uncommon. Example:

"Chrōnŏnhōtŏnthōlŏgōs thĕ Grēat,
Godlike in a barrow kept his state."

5. The fifth Trochaic species is likewise uncommon; and, as a Bowbellian would say, "uncommon" ugly. It contains *five* trochees: as,

"Hēre lĭes Mārў, wīfe ŏf Thōmăs Cārtĕr,
Who to typhus fever proved a martyr."

"THE NASTY LITTLE SQUALLING BRAT"

"Would you, you disagreeable old Bachelor?"

These are a specimen of the "uncouth rhymes" so touchingly alluded to by Gray.

6. The sixth form of the English Trochaic is a line of six trochees: as,

"Mōst bĕwītchĭng dāmsĕl, charmĭng Ārăbēllă,
Prithee, cast an eye of pity on a fellow."

The Dactylic measure is extremely uncommon. The following may be considered an example of one species of it:

"Cēliă thĕ crūĕl, rĕsōlv'd nŏt tŏ mārrў sŏon,
Boasts of a heart like a fortified garrison,
Bulwarks and battlements keeping the *beaux* all off,
Shot from within knocking lovers like foes all off."

Anapæstic verses are of various kinds.

1. The shortest anapæstic verse is a single anapæst: as,

"Ĭn thĕ glāss
There's an ass."

This measure, after all, is ambiguous; for if the stress of the voice be laid on the first and third syllables, it becomes trochaic. Perhaps, therefore, it is best to consider the first form of our Anapæstic verse, as made up of two anapæsts: as,

"Sĕt ă schōolbŏy ăt wōrk
With a knife and a fork."

And here, if you like, you may have another short syllable: as,

> "Ănd hŏw sōon thĕ yoŭng glŭttŏn
> Will astonish your mutton!"

2. The second species consists of three anapæsts: as,

> "Ămărȳllĭs wăs slēndĕr ănd tāll,
> Colin Clodpole was dumpy and fat;
> And tho' *she* did'n't like him at all,
> Yet he doted on *her* for all that."

This metre is sometimes donominated sing-song.

3. The third kind of *English* Anapæstics may be very well exemplified by an *Irish* song:

> "Hăve yŏu ē'er hăd thĕ lūck tŏ sĕe Dōnnȳbrŏok Fāir?"

It consists, as will have been observed, of four anapæsts. Sometimes it admits of a short syllable at the end of the verse: as,

> "Ĭn thĕ dēad ŏf thĕ nīght, whĕn wĭth dīre cătĕrwāulĭng
> Of grimalkins in chorus the house-tops resound;
> All insensibly drunk, and unconsciously sprawling
> In the kennel, how pleasant it is to be found!"

The various specimens of versification of which examples have been given, may be improved and varied by the admission of secondary feet into their composition; but as we are not writing an Art of Poetry, we cannot afford to show how: particularly as the only way, after all, of acquiring a real knowledge of the structure of English verse, is by extensive reading. Besides, there yet remain a few Directions for Poetical Beginners, which we feel ourselves called upon to give, and for which, if we do not take care, we shall not have room.

The commencement of a poet's career is usually the writing of *nonsense* verses. The nonsense of these compositions is very often unintentional; but sometimes words are put together avowedly without regard to sense, and with no other view than that of acquiring a familiarity with metrical arrangement: as,

> "Approach, disdain, involuntary, tell."

But this is dry work. It may be necessary to compose in this way just at first, but in our opinion, there is a good and a bad taste to be displayed even in writing nonsense verses; that is, verses which really deserve that name. We recommend the young poet to make it his aim to render his nonsense as PERFECT as possible. He will find many bright examples to follow in the world of literature: but perhaps, for the present, he will put up with our own.

> "Conclusive tenderness; fraternal grog,
> Tidy conjunction; adamantine bog,
> Impetuous, arrant toadstool; Thundering quince,
> Repentant dog-star, inessential Prince
> Expound. Pre-Adamite eventful gun,

Crush retribution, currant-jelly, pun.
Oh! eligible Darkness, fender, sting
Heav'n-born Insanity, courageous thing.
Intending, bending, scouring, piercing all,
Death like pomatum, tea, and crabs must fall."

A very good method of making nonsense verses, consists in taking bits, selected here and there at random, out of some particular poet, or phrases in his style, and then putting them together with a few additions of your own *secundùm artem*. Sometimes, however, it answers very well to copy a page or so of an author word for word. Nonsense verses composed in this manner, form not only a beneficial exercise, but are also very useful for insertion in young ladies' albums; as they can be made without much trouble, and when made, are not only thought just as well of as the most sensible productions would be, but very often cried over into the bargain, as affecting and pathetic.

EXAMPLE.

THE OCEAN WANDERER.

"Bright breaks the warrior o'er the ocean wave
Through realms that rove not, clouds that cannot save,
Sinks in the sunshine; dazzles o'er the tomb,
And mocks the mutiny of Memory's gloom.
Oh! who can feel the crimson ecstasy
That soothes with bickering jar the Glorious Free?
O'er the high rock the foam of gladness throws,
While star-beams lull Vesuvius to repose:
Girds the white spray, and in the blue lagoon,
Weeps like a walrus o'er the waning moon?
Who can declare?—not thou, pervading boy
Whom pibrochs pierce not, crystals cannot cloy;—
Not thou, soft Architect of silvery gleams,
Whose soul would simmer in Hesperian streams,
Th' exhaustless fire—the bosom's azure bliss,
That hurtles, life-like, o'er a scene like this;—
Defies the distant agony of Day—
And sweeps o'er hecatombs—away! away!
Say, shall Destruction's lava load the gale,
The furnace quiver, and the mountain quail?
Say, shall the son of Sympathy pretend
His cedar fragrance with our Chief's to blend?
There, where the gnarled monuments of sand
Howl their dark whirlwinds to the levin brand;
Where avalanches wail, and green Distress
Sweeps o'er the pallid beak of loveliness:
Where melancholy Sulphur holds her sway;
And cliffs of Conscience tremble, and obey;

> And where Tartarean rattle-snakes expire,
> Twisting like tendrils of a hero's pyre?
> No! dancing in the meteor's hall of power,
> See, Genius ponders o'er Affection's tower!
> A form of thund'ring import soars on high,
> Hark! 'tis the gore of infant melody:
> No more shall verdant Innocence amuse
> The lips that death-fraught Indignation glues;—
> Tempests shall teach the trackless tide of thought,
> That undistinguish'd senselessness is nought:
> Freedom shall glare; and oh! ye links divine,
> The Poet's heart shall quiver in the brine."

Suppose we try another metre.

> "The Spirit saw and smiled,
> And an interminable radiance glowed
> Throughout her lucid frame;
> There rose within her soul
> A wild unspeakable intelligence,
> A sweet and gentle light,
> Which through her eyes in countless flashes shone
> Intolerably bright;
> Like to an infinite multitude of stars
> Gemming the arch of Heaven;
> Or, rather, like the shining balls that come
> Out of a Roman candle."

However, we are not quite sure that, with the exception of the two last lines, we have not quoted the rest of the foregoing example from memory.

It were manifestly culpable to make no mention, in a work of this sort, of certain measures which are especially and essentially of a comic nature. Some of these have been already adverted to, but two principal varieties yet remain to be considered.

1. Measures taken from the Latin, in which the structure of the ancient verse, as far as the number and arrangement of the feet are concerned, is preserved, but the quantity of which is regulated in accordance with the spirit of our own language. The character of such verses will be best displayed by employing them on sentimental or serious subjects. Take, for example, Long and Short, or Hexameter and Pentameter verses.

> "Jūlĭă, gīrl ŏf mў heārt, ĭs thăn jēssămĭne swēetĕr, ŏr frĕsh mēads
> Hāy-cŏvĕr'd; whāt rōse tīnts thōse ŏn hĕr chēeks, thăt flŏurīsh,
> Approach? those bright eyes, what stars, what glittering dew-drops?
> And oh! what Parian marble, or snow, that bosom?
> If she my love return, what bliss will be greater than mine; but
> What more deep sadness if she reprove my passion?
> Either a bridegroom proud yon ivy-clad church shall receive me

Soon; or the cold church-yard me with its turf shall cover."

Or the Sapphic metre, of which the late Mr. Canning's "Knife-Grinder" is so brilliant an example. Sappho, fair reader, was a poetess, who made love-verses which could be actually scanned. History relates that, for the sake of some unprincipled or unfeeling fellow, she committed *felo de se*.

> "'Ī căn ēndūre thīs crŭĕl pāin nŏ lōngēr;
> Fare ye well, blue skies, rivers, fields, and song-birds!'
> Thus the youth spoke: and adding, 'Oh, Jemima!'
> Plunged in the billow!"

"OH, JEMIMA!"

2. Measures reducible to no rule, or Doggrel. Sternhold and Hopkins, of whom such honourable mention has been made above, were illustrious as Doggrel writers. They have been somewhat eclipsed, however, by their modern successors, Nicholas Brady and Nahum Tate, who may, perhaps, be safely pronounced the chief of *uninspired* bards.

Original composers in this description of verse are often not much more particular about Syntax,—and we might add Orthography,—than they are about
Prosody. The following extract from an unpublished satire on the singing of a
country catch-club, is a tolerably fair specimen of English Doggrel:—

> "A gentleman, who was passing by,
> Was very much amazed at what they were going to try,
> Said, 'Hear their voices, how they sing,
> How badly they all chime in!'
> After such singing, what do you think of us,
> To send forth sounds of mirthfulness?"

Doggrel is commonly used by anonymous poets for the purpose of embody-
ing the moral reflections which a homicide or an execution excites in the sensitive
mind. It is likewise the metre in which the imaginative sempstress pours forth the
feelings of her bosom. May we hope that our remarks on Prosody will in some little degree tend to facilitate, perhaps to improve, the future treatment of those two
deeply interesting subjects—Love and Murder?

LOVE AND MURDER

CHAPTER III.
PUNCTUATION.

"Mind your stops." This is one of the earliest maxims inculcated by the instructors of youth. Hence it is clear that the subject of Punctuation is an important one; but inasmuch as the reader, who has arrived at the present page, has either not understood a word that he has been reading, or else knows as much about the matter as we can tell him, we fear that a long dissertation concerning periods, commas, and so on, would only serve to embarrass his progress in learning with useless STOPS. We shall, therefore, confine ourselves to that notice of Punctuation, and that only, which the peculiar nature of our work may require.

STANDING ON POINTS

First, it may be remarked, that the notes *of admiration* which we so often hear in theatres, may be called *notes of hand*. Secondly, that *notes of interrogation* are not at all like *bank notes*; although they are largely uttered in *Banco Reginæ*. Let us now proceed with our subject.

It is both absurd and inconvenient to stand upon *points*.

Of how much consequence, however, Punctuation is, the student may form some idea, by considering the different effects which a piece of poetry, for instance, which he has been accustomed to regard as sublime or beautiful, will have, when liberties are taken with it in that respect.

Imagine an actor commencing Hamlet's famous soliloquy, thus:—

"To be; or not to be that is. The question," &c.

Or saying, in the person of Duncan, in Macbeth:

"This castle hath a pleasant seat, the air."

Or as the usurper himself, exclaiming,

"The devil damn thee black, thou cream-faced loon!
Where got'st thou that goose? Look!"

"WHERE GOT'ST THOU THAT GOOSE?"

Crying, as Romeo,

> "It is my lady O! It is my love!"

Or in the character of Norval, in the tragedy of Douglas, giving this account of himself and his origin:

> "My name is Norval. On the Grampian hills
> My father feeds."

In short, Punctuation is the soul of Grammar, as Punctuality is that of business.

Perhaps somebody or other may take advantage of what we have said, to prove both Punctuation and Punctuality *immaterial*. No matter.

How very punctual the present Ministers are! how well they *keep their appointments*!

We have now said as much as we think it necessary to say on the head of English Grammar. We shall conclude our labours with an "Address to Young Students;" and as to the question, what that has to do with our subject, we shall leave it to be settled by Lindley Murray, whose example, in this respect, we follow. All we shall observe is, that in our opinion, advice concerning manners stands in the same relation to a Comic English Grammar, as instruction in morals does to a Serious one. For the remarks which it will now be our business to make, we bespeak the indulgence of our elder readers, and the attention of such as are of tender age.

ADDRESS TO YOUNG STUDENTS.

Young Gentlemen,

Having attentively perused the foregoing pages, you will be desirous, it is to be presumed, of carrying still further those comical pursuits in which, with both pleasure and profit to yourselves, you have been lately engaged. Should such be your laudable intention, you will learn, with feelings of lively satisfaction, that it is one, in the accomplishment of which, thanks to Modern Taste, you will find encouragement at every step. The literature of the day is professedly comic, and of the few works which are not made ludicrous by the design of their authors, the majority are rendered so in spite of it. In the course of your reading, however, you will be frequently brought into contact with hackney-coachmen, cabmen, lackeys, turnkeys, thieves, lawyers' clerks, medical students, and other people of that description, who are all very amusing when properly viewed, as the monkeys and such like animals at the Zoological Gardens are, when you look at them through the bars of their cage. But too great familiarity with persons of this class is sure to breed contempt, not for them and their manners, but for the usages and modes of expression adopted in parlours and drawing-rooms, that is to say, in good society. Nay, it is very likely to cause those who indulge in it to learn various tricks and eccentricities, both of behaviour and speech, for "It is certain, that either wise bearing or ignorant carriage is caught, as men take diseases, one of another." Shakspere.

Beset thus, as you will necessarily be, by perils and dangers in your wanderings amid the fields of Comicality, you will derive great advantage from knowing before-hand what you are likely to meet with, and what it will be incumbent on you to avoid. It is to furnish you with this information that the following hints and instructions are intended.

Be careful, when you hear yourself called by name, to reply "Here I am," and not "Here you are," an error into which you are very likely to be led by the perusal of existing authors.

When you partake, if it be your habit to do so, of the beverage called porter, drink it as you would water, or any other liquid. Do not wink your eye, or nod sideways to your companion; such actions, especially when preceded by blowing away the foam which collects on the top of the vessel, being exceedingly inelegant: and in order that you may not be incommoded by this foam or froth, always pour the fluid gently into a tumbler, instead of drinking it out of the metallic tankard in which it is usually brought to you.

In asking for malt liquor generally, never request the waiter to "draw it mild;" and do not, on any occasion, be guilty of using the same phrase in a metaphorical sense, that is to say, as a substitute, for "Do it quietly." "Be gentle," and the like.

Never exhort young ladies, during a quadrille, to "fake away," or to "flare up," for they, being unacquainted with the meaning of such terms, will naturally conclude that it is an improper one.

Call all articles of dress by their proper names. What delight can be found by a thinking mind in designating a hat as a tile, trousers, kickseys, a neckerchief, a fogle, or a choker; or a great coat, an upper Benjamin? And never speak of clothes, collectively, as togs or toggery.

Avoid inquiries after the health of another person's mother, using that word synonymously with Mamma, to denote a female parent. Though you may be really innocent of any intention to be rude, your motives may very possibly be misconstrued. Remember, also, on no account to put questions, either to friends or strangers, respecting the quantity of soap in their possession.

Should it be necessary for you to speak of some one smoking tobacco, do not call that substance a weed, or the act of using it "blowing a cloud."

When an acquaintance pays you a visit, take care, in rising to receive him, not to appear to be washing your hands, and, should you be engaged in writing at the time, place your pen on the table, or in the inkstand, and not behind your ear.

Observe, when your tailor comes to measure you, the way in which he wears his hair, and should your own style in this particular unfortunately resemble his, be sure to alter it immediately.

Never dance *à la cuisinière*, that is to say, do not cut capers.

Eschew large shirt pins.

Be not guilty of patent leather boots.

Never say "Ma'am" or "Miss," in addressing a young lady. If you cannot contrive to speak to her without doing so, say nothing.

In conversation, especially in female society, beware of indulging in jocose expressions, or witticisms, on the subject of executions. If it be necessary to remark that such and such a person expiated his crimes on the scaffold, content yourself with simply mentioning the circumstance, and do not make any attempt to illustrate your meaning by dropping your head on your right shoulder, and jerking up your neckcloth under your left ear.

Never, under any circumstances, let the abbreviation "gent." for gentleman, escape the enclosure of your teeth. Above all things, for the sake of whatever you hold most dear, never say "me and another gent."

It may happen, that a youthful acquaintance may so far forget himself as to talk of giving another "monkey's allowance, more kicks than half-pence." You, of course, will never dream of giving utterance to such language, nor will any inducement, it is to be hoped, ever prevail upon you to say, as an unthinking young friend once did, hearing the above threat made, "that you prefer *kicks* (meaning thereby sixpences) to half-pence." In general avoid all low wit.

When you receive a coin of any kind, deposit it at once in your pocket, without the needless preliminary of furling it in the air.

Never ask a gentleman how much he has a-year.

In speaking of a person of your own age, or of an elderly gentleman, do not say, Old So-and-So, but So-and-so, or *Mr.* So-and-so, as the case may be: and have no nicknames for each other. We were much horrified not long since, by hearing a great coarse fellow, in a leathern hat and fustian jacket, exclaim, turning round to his companion, "Now, then, come along, old Blokey!"

When you have got a cold in the head and weak eyes, do not go and call on young ladies.

Do not eat gravy with a knife, for fear those about you should suppose you to be going to commit suicide.

In offering to help a person at dinner, do not say, "Allow me to *assist* you." When you ask people what wine they will take, never say, "What'll you have?" or, "What'll you *do it in*?"

If you are talking to a clergyman about another member of the clerical profession, adopt some other method of describing his avocation than that of saying, "I believe he is in your line."

Do not recommend an omelet to a lady, as a good *article*.

Be cautious not to use the initial letter of a person's surname, in mentioning or in addressing him. For instance, never think of saying, "Mrs. Hobbs, pray, how is Mr. H.?"

We here approach the conclusion of our labours. Young gentlemen, once more it is earnestly requested that you will give your careful attention to the rules and admonitions which have been above laid down for your guidance. We might have given a great many more; but we hope that the spirit of our instructions will enable the diligent youth to supply, by observation and reflection, that which, for obvious reasons, we have necessarily left unsaid. And now we bid you farewell. That you may never have the misfortune of entering, with splashed boots, a drawing-room full of ladies; that you may never, having been engaged in a brawl on the previous evening, meet, with a black eye, the object of your affections the next morning; that you may never, in a moment of agitation, omit the aspirate, or use it when you ought not; that your laundress may always do justice to your linen; and your tailor make your clothes well, and send them home in due time; that your braces may never give way during a waltz; that you may never, sitting in a strong light at a large dinner-party, suddenly remember that you have not shaved for two days; that your hands and face may ever be free from tan, chaps, freckles, pimples, brandy-blossoms, and all other disfigurements; that you may never be either inelegantly fat, or ridiculously lean; and finally, that you may always have plenty to eat, plenty to drink, and plenty to laugh at, we earnestly and sincerely wish. And should your lot in life be other than fortunate, we can only say, that we advise you to bear it with patience; to cultivate Comic Philosophy; and to look upon your troubles as a joke.

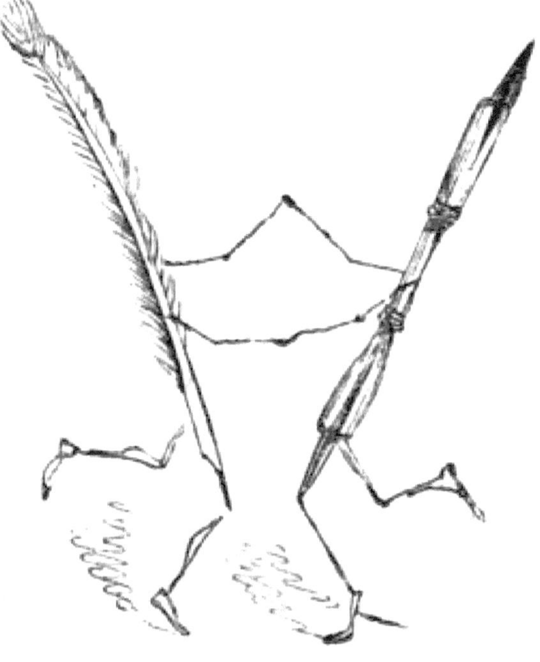

VIVAT REGINA!

THE END.

Lector House believes that a society develops through a two-fold approach of continuous learning and adaptation, which is derived from the study of classic literary works spread across the historic timeline of literature records. Therefore, we aim at reviving, repairing and redeveloping all those inaccessible or damaged but historically as well as culturally important literature across subjects so that the future generations may have an opportunity to study and learn from past works to embark upon a journey of creating a better future.

This book is a result of an effort made by Lector House towards making a contribution to the preservation and repair of original ancient works which might hold historical significance to the approach of continuous learning across subjects.

HAPPY READING & LEARNING!

LECTOR HOUSE LLP
E-MAIL: lectorpublishing@gmail.com